A Little Better than Plumb

A Little Better than Plumb

The Biography of a House

Henry and Janice Holt Giles

Foreword by L. Elisabeth Beattie
Illustrations by Pansy Wilcoxson Phillips

THE UNIVERSITY PRESS OF KENTUCKY

Published in 1995 by The University Press of Kentucky
Foreword copyright © 1995 by The University Press of Kentucky

Scholarly publisher for the Commonwealth,
serving Bellarmine College, Berea College, Centre
College of Kentucky, Eastern Kentucky University,
The Filson Club, Georgetown College, Kentucky
Historical Society, Kentucky State University,
Morehead State University, Murray State University,
Northern Kentucky University, Transylvania University,
University of Kentucky, University of Louisville,
and Western Kentucky University.
Editorial and Sales Offices: Lexington, Kentucky 40508-4008

Library of Congress Cataloging-in-Publication Data
Giles, Henry, 1916-1986.
  A little better than plumb : the biography of a house / Henry and
Janice Holt Giles ; foreword by L. Elisabeth Beattie ; illustrations
by Pansy Wilcoxson Phillips.
       p. cm.
  Originally published: Boston : Houghton Mifflin, © 1963.
  ISBN 0-8131-1897-2 (acid-free paper). —ISBN 0-8131-0833-0 (pbk.)
  1. Country life—Kentucky—Adair County. 2. Giles, Henry,
1916-1986. 3. Giles, Janice Holt. 4. Log Cabins—Design and
construction—Anecdotes. I. Giles, Janice Holt. II. Title.
F457.A3G55   1995
976.9'675—dc20   95-7889

This book is printed on acid-free recycled paper meeting
the requirements of the American National Standard
for Permanence of Paper for Printed Library Materials.

♾ ♼

To those for whom
this old house was really built

The Grandsons

Bart, Mike, and Scott Hancock

Contents

Foreword

Thirty-two years separate the first publication of *A Little Better than Plumb* from the date of this reprint, but Henry and Janice Holt Giles's biography of a house retains the wry, rough-edged humor that gained it popularity with an earlier generation of readers. In this memoir Janice Holt Giles, author of such historical fiction classics as *The Enduring Hills, Miss Willie,* and *The Kentuckians,* and her husband, Henry Giles, who wrote *Harbin's Ridge,* collaborated on a book in which the house they construct serves as a metaphor for the marriage they build. Warped boards parallel egos bent hilariously out of shape by wallpaper willing to sag but not hang, or by windows whose crooked panes cause their owners pains of another sort.

Janice Holt Moore, an Arkansas native who spent the final forty years of her life in Kentucky, was secretary to the dean of the Presbyterian Seminary in Louisville when she met Henry Giles, a soldier and her husband-to-be, in 1943 on a bus out of Bowling Green. After their marriage in 1945, they lived in Louisville for four years, then moved to Spout Springs, close to Knifely, in Adair County. *A Little Better than Plumb* traces the trials and tribulations of a city couple's coming to terms with the fissure between their romantic notions of the simple life and the stark reality of pioneering. Having sold her first novel, Janice wanted to retire to the country to

write. And so she and her husband did just that, as Janice
recorded in her first memoir, *40 Acres and No Mule*. With
fifty dollars to their names they decided to refurbish their first
rural dwelling, a fiasco that gained them respect for their
neighbors' know-how, as well as an exact measure of their own
shortcomings.

Janice writes, "The truth is that not since the first man
pushed a pointed stick around in some dirt and planted a
handful of seeds have there been sadder or unhappier farmers than Mr. G. and I were. And we persisted in this insanity for three long years."

Instead of retreating to urbanity, Janice and Mr. G. em-
braced what they would agree was the quintessence of insanity by building a log cabin on the banks of the Green River.
The Wife designed "The Plan" (a blueprint she believed Mr.
G. burned out of sheer frustration toward the end of the construction process), and the Husband executed it. As might
be expected, The Plan and the completed house bore little
resemblance to each other.

Problems with walls and logs and the roof were one thing;
difficulties with weeds and mice and snakes presented snafus
of other dimensions. Through the recollection of it all Janice
Holt Giles keeps her readers laughing, as does Mr. G. in the
chapters he pens from his equally skewed perspective.

The coauthored nature of the text enables its tone to work.
Janice's sometimes less-than-gentle jabs at Mr. G.'s roared re-
sponses to her remarks, and his reports of his wife's naive
requests, might sound petty—and both spouses might seem
mean-spirited and petulant—were it not for the book's dual
authorship. Mr. G. at his wife's hand constitutes a character
of single-minded garrulousness, creating enormous comic ef-

fect at the expense of his gentler nature. But with his own sensible and sensitive choice of diction he erupts into a well-rounded man who indeed might be goaded into much of his ill temper. And Janice, who, by her own admission, arrived armed for rural living less with ability for roughing it than with idealistic attitudes, gets goosed a bit by her gander in Mr. G.'s chapters, just as she pecks at him in hers.

The bickering of Mr. and Mrs. Giles is the book's very mortar; it binds every chapter with the wit that makes *A Little Better than Plumb* a text about the stuff that sustains human nature more than about a frame that supports a sole house. In fact, reading the Gileses' account of their botched building processes is rather like watching episode after episode of the sitcom classic *The Honeymooners*. Janice and Henry Giles and Alice and Ralph Kramden survive for the same reasons: each couple thrives on that peculiar, curiously intellectual form of loveplay in which only the witty can participate. But trading barbs elevates mundane existences and tedious tasks into imaginative exchanges. The world takes on a comic cast and the players' lives emerge as suddenly, spectacularly colorful. So the book's dual authorship and humorous tone elevate it from the realm of isolated experience to the plane of shared humanity.

Since the Gileses' book first appeared, the women's movement has caused writers and editors to evaluate language more carefully for sexist intent and to examine ideas themselves for their inclusion of archaic assumptions concerning gender roles. *A Little Better than Plumb* could be criticized by today's readers for including references and attitudes now considered gauche. But such readers would themselves retain the greater insensitivity, for the Gileses' words simply reconstruct, instead of advocate after the fact, the socially accepted gender role differences of an earlier generation. And the careful reader will note that their Punch and Judy style of verbal fencing bespeaks an equality of mind and a mutual regard that far outstrip any traditional tasks each performs.

At the book's end Janice Holt Giles asks, "How do you reorient the heart?" She continues, "We determined to set it all down, the story of a house conceived in nostalgia, born in hope, nurtured in determination, nourished in loves, vexations, frustrations, joy, laughter, and triumph, matured in despair, and doomed by progress." As she concludes, "We meant to leave it an epitaph." Perhaps the Gileses' house by Green River, the home with a living room that encompasses the logs of an ancient African-American church, commemorates all those entities and emotions to which Mrs. G. refers. Ultimately, *A Little Better than Plumb* is an epitaph also to Janice, who died in 1979, to Henry, who died in 1986, and to the marriage they built together.

L. ELISABETH BEATTIE

Chapter 1
Creeks Don't Run Uphill

MISTER G. holds with the theory that husbands generally have an easier time of it, wives are at least temporarily happier, and there is less sturm-und-drang all around if, within reason, wives are allowed to believe they have their own way.

"It does no great harm," I heard him confide to a newly wedded friend one day, "and it keeps the peace."

"Peace by appeasement," his friend scoffed.

"Not so," my spouse stoutly denied, "peace by strategy. Think of it this way. Is it earth-shaking whether the living room walls are blue or yellow? Is it universally important where the rosebushes are planted? Will it start a war if the wall-to-wall carpeting is acrilan instead of wool? And will Latin-American relationships be disturbed if you have to wear a tie you don't like?"

Loftily the young benedict replied, "Perhaps not. But just the same I intend to be the man of *my* family."

"You think I'm not?" Mister G. murmured. "That's the secret of my policy. On small things, my friend, give. Give like an elastic band. Give till it hurts. Save your strength for the issues that matter. On really important things assert yourself firmly and strongly. On really important things, stand up on your hind legs and roar. Put up with no shilly-shallying on the really important things. Bellow like the bull of Bashan and brook no interference."

The young friend pondered. "What," he asked then, a trifle timorously, "*are* the important things?"

Mister G. settled deeply and delightedly into his chair. "First," he began . . . and I fled. I didn't need to hear more. I remembered all too well the times he had roared like the bull of Bashan, and what about. I knew what was coming.

It was a matter of breakfast the first time.

When I met Mister G. in 1943 my household had for a good many years consisted of myself and my daughter, Libby, and we lived in Louisville, Kentucky. We had come from the southwest in 1940 when I was offered a position as secretarial assistant to the dean of the Louisville Presbyterian Seminary. It proved to be a wise and happy move, for I had an almost ideal working situation and Libby loved everything but the weather about Kentucky.

By 1943 she was a freshman at the University of Louisville, beautiful as a gypsy and as dizzyingly heady as a bottle of champagne. This could have gone on forever as far as I was concerned but my child, naturally, had her own life to live and in the summer of 1944 she bravely married her young man six weeks before he flew across the Atlantic to join the 15th Air Corps in Italy.

A statement I sometimes make too offhandedly is that I was not married until after my daughter was married. This causes a double take occasionally. But I assume it's understood she was born of a prior marriage. Younger and more adventurous, Libby and Nash did not wait as Mister G. and I did for the war to end. I think I would have waited, however, under any circumstances for her marriage, for however fond of Mister G. I was, a stepfather, while she was still at home and at her age, was something I would have thought about a long, long time before giving her. Had I met Mister G. earlier, when he could have been a real father to her, I shouldn't have hesitated a second.

But by the time he and I knew each other well enough to begin to think of marriage, Libby was almost nineteen and deeply in love with Nash Hancock, a young man of whom I heartily approved. In any event it all became academic when Mister G. was picked up willy-nilly, with no forewarning, and deposited in England to await the invasion. Libby dashed out to Tucson to marry and came home for another winter with me when Nash went to Italy. It was two years before I saw Mister G. again.

At any rate, our years of a two-woman household had got me out of the habit of a hearty breakfast. We two females drank a glass of fruit juice, nibbled at toast and sipped at coffee. For a real splurge on Sunday morning we added jelly to the toast.

Dimly realizing a man needed more rib-sticking fare, in the early months of marriage to Mister G. I gave him an egg also. It took only one month of this delicate morning repast for him to shove his plate back one day and set his mouth mulishly and raise his voice sharply. "I want," he said clearly, distinctly and positively, "hot biscuits for breakfast. I want at least two eggs, with bacon, sausage or ham. I don't want cereal or toast or fruit juice. I also want full-bodied jams or preserves. And," he added, "I'd appreciate cream gravy."

Naturally I knew he had grown up on a farm and everybody knows farmers have lusty appetites. But we lived in the city, in a second-floor apartment, without so much as a window box to plow. I made the mistake of not taking him seriously. "Oh, come now, not *every* morning," I said archly.

"*Every morning*," he insisted, and he rose from his chair. It seemed to me he rose and rose to an interminable height until he towered over me threateningly. In fact, he did threaten. "If you serve me any more of that crap you call food I'll throw it out the window!"

Then he strode out of the kitchen and left me to meditate upon this sudden turn of affairs. There was no doubting he meant it and there was no doubting he would heave the crap I called food right out the window if I put it before him again. I was tempted to try it just to see if he would, but for the sake of the defenseless pedestrians below, I told myself . . .

Well, come hell or high water, for eighteen years Mister G. has had hot biscuits, two eggs, bacon, ham or sausage, jam or preserves (and frequently both) *and* cream gravy for breakfast. I estimate that as of now I have made one hundred and thirty-one thousand, four hundred eighty-four biscuits, cooked thirteen thousand eggs, fried six thousand and seventy pounds of bacon, one hundred hams, five thousand pounds of sausage, and stirred up at least ten thousand gallons of cream gravy! Only an illness severe enough to keep me from lifting my head from the pillow prevents me from cooking this harvest-hand banquet every morning of my life.

So — breakfast was undoubtedly first on Mister G.'s list of

really important things about which a man should rear back on his hind legs and roar. I wondered if I should warn the young wife, but decided not to. I thought she probably wouldn't have believed me anyhow.

I had not forgotten, either, the time a coffee table was seized in Olympian rage and hurled across the room, to be followed immediately by a milk glass bowl, with lid, full of salted nuts. It was quite a sight to see and there was quite a mess and some things were never the same again. The coffee table, for instance. The right front leg acquired a wobble from which it never recovered no matter how much tightening or bracing or wiring was applied to it. The milk glass bowl was a shattering loss and my nerves were left a trifle undone also.

A peaceful man's rebellious and sudden assertion of himself so violently is something awesome to behold and witnessing it for the first time I wasn't sure I wouldn't find myself flying through the air next. That I didn't was probably due only to the fact that Mister G. doesn't actually hold with belting his wife no matter how apoplectic he may be or how itchingly he may long to do so. But I have remained confident I had a near miss.

All I did was to ask, innocently, where he had been for eight hours one January Sunday when a blizzard straight from the Hudson's Bay ice fields was raging. When he had left at eight o'clock that morning it was to drive three miles to the country store to pick up the Sunday paper. Normally he was gone about thirty minutes.

At the end of two hours I was mildly apprehensive. It was snowing thicker and thicker all the time, the wind had got up to a howl, and there was a steep hill he had to drive *down* to reach the store and back up to get home. It was possible,

I thought, and reasonable enough it seemed to me, he might have gone into a ditch.

At the end of four hours I was more than mildly apprehensive, I was wildly worried and positive by now that he had gone into a ditch. 'While walking the floor and biting my nails and twisting my forelock, helpless without a telephone, my imagination ran riot and I could see him struggling to get the car free, freezing his ears and his fingers and his toes. Against my will there even crept in the picture of him pinned, maybe, beneath an overturned car.

At the end of eight hours I was ready for a straightjacket, as certain now as I had ever been of anything in my life that he had been killed, buried in the snow, passed by unseen and allowed to freeze stiff. I was even dressed, ready to accompany whatever kind friend would eventually come to tell me the awful news, to the hospital or funeral home!

I never did find out precisely how he spent those eight hours, but I did find out, once and for all, that nothing so incenses a husband as to have a tearfully anxious wife jump at him and scream, *"Where have you been?"* when he returns, slightly guilty as well as mellow, from a snuck-out time with the boys!

Mister G. bellowed at me to mind my own business before he began heaving the furniture about.

Now, in good voice, I have a bellow that can call home the cows myself, and when I could get my breath I was in the best voice of my life. If my bellow didn't call home a few of the neighbor's cows as well as our own, I'd be mortally surprised. To this good day Mister G. insists he learned that day what was meant by the phrase "make the rafters ring."

He only bellowed once, but I hate to remember how long

I shrieked like a fishwife. He must have thought he had pulled out the stopper.

At any rate when peace had been restored there was a quiet meeting of minds in which it was agreed that Mister G. could roar if he pleased and if he didn't mind being roared back at, but there would be no more throwing furniture about. It was also agreed that Mister G. had every right to go out with the boys when he pleased, but he ought to say so beforehand.

This may not have been quite fair of me, because since we have no telephones in our neck of the woods he sometimes has to drive home to tell me he is going right back where he came from and be gone another two or three hours. But I was too shook to be wholly fair and with some give and take it has worked out pretty well. Usually I give him a couple of hours leeway, and he takes it.

I didn't think this was a fit story to tell the young wife, either. It would only horrify her, and she would be certain her John would never behave so. Let her cross her own bridges as she came to them. But right now, I was positive, my Mister G., one of the Lord's best works of art, was telling her John to stand up on his hind legs and roar for his right to some freedom and independence. I longed to tell her, don't give him a mean and niggardly inch. Just give him the whole rope and he'll follow it home in time.

I particularly remember two other occasions when Mister G. has asserted himself.

I had written a novel. It had been accepted by a publisher. In sublime ignorance and supreme self-confidence, we quit our jobs in the city, spent all our savings on a forty-acre tract of timber hilariously miscalled a farm, and moved to the ridge. It makes me shudder now to remember how confidently we believed we could earn our way by writing! So few writers do. But we didn't know that. And we wanted to be full-time writers. So we just hitched up and moved to the country.

We were the two deadest-broke people in Kentucky for a while, but that first summer on our forty acres we were having what I thought was a rather larky time. There were no pressures, no schedules, no buses and crowds and pavements and office routines, no real obligations or duties, and plenty of time for writing. Of course there was no money either but that didn't bother us too much because there was a foreseeable end to money shortage when book royalties began to come rolling in. A year of short shrift by deliberate choice can easily be weathered and even enjoyed.

To me the whole thing was a delightful adventure and all that summer in a blissfully exhilarated state I tagged like a faithful dog at Mister G.'s heels as he explored and surveyed our forty acres. He had known them all his life, traipsed and hunted over them, but now that he owned them he wanted to make a new acquaintance with them on different terms. Thirty of the forty acres were hills and hollows and I've forgotten now whether it was three hills and two hollows or the other way around, but no matter, in bluejeans and sneakers, my hair tied up in a bandanna, I trudged up and down them with him.

Not one to impart information unsolicited, he must have been pestered almost out of his wits by my eternal questions but he was patient and tried to teach me all the new things of the woods. It isn't his fault that I'm still as likely to pluck a hickory seedling and call it ginseng as not, or that I still get my trees mixed and my birds mixed and my snakes mixed; or that Green River flows just as due east to me as it did the first time I ever saw it when he has told me at least a thousand times it flows west. Or that an adz looks just like a grubbing hoe to me, and I am still guilty of using one to dig up the bulbs.

We had some wonderful times. I paddled the old rowboat for him while he fished on the river, trailed him over the old paths, cooked our grand garden food on an ancient kerosene stove, slept dreamlessly in the attic, grew freckled and brown and developed some good stout leg and arm muscles.

But my mother has a genius for sniffing out interesting shifts and nuances in the lives of her children and for wanting to see firsthand what they're up to. If she had been appalled when her oldest had suddenly given up security and comfort to move to the country, she hadn't said so. She just bided her time for a few months, then wrote she was coming for a short visit. And she took good care not to give me time to reply and say, not yet, please. She would arrive, she said . . . please meet her.

Wildly I wondered exactly what I had written her about the way we were living. How much had I glamorized it? I knew I had made it sound gay and interesting and exciting and that I had deliberately glossed over the outhouse and the dug well, and the way I did our washing on a scrubboard, by hand, as well as all our other little forced economies. We rolled our own cigarettes and ate almost wholly out of the garden. The only meat we ever had was an occasional chicken Mister G.'s mother gave us, the fish he caught and the squirrels he killed.

For the first time I felt uncomfortable about the way we were living. I doubted she would think the tall, gaunt, unpainted shack we called home was very larky. There were

two rooms below and a big, unfloored, unfinished attic overhead. Remembering that when we rolled out of bed each
morning we hopped rafters to reach the stairs I quickly
decided to give her a bed downstairs. Her hopping days
might be over.

We wrestled a small bed down the laddery stairs and set
it up. Then I made the mistake of taking a good look at the
walls. The myopic state in which I usually go around had
kept me from really seeing them before. But now my eyes
were opened. The house had been built of green lumber
which had seasoned wryly, opening a lot of cracks. Because
it rained in the cracks we had collected an untold number of
cardboard cartons, flattened them and nailed them over the
cracks. We also hoped they would keep out some of the cold
north wind when winter came. But they were not very
sightly and there was no fooling myself about them.

The floors loomed up at me then, rough and splintery and
uneven, and the whipsawed, unplaned window frames and
doors. Distressed, I thought of only one answer — paint, wallpaper, and the cheapest linoleum rugs to be found.

I should have had more faith in my mother. There never
was a time when she hadn't thoroughly enjoyed camping out
and roughing it. Furthermore, she was no novice at it. I was
just playing at pioneering that year but she had actually done
it in the rough country of eastern Oklahoma when she had
gone there, around the turn of the century, as a bride. But
some kind of stubborn pride invaded me and since we had
three days before she was to arrive I had to stew around and
harry us both and bustle and clean and paint and paper.

We had less than fifty dollars in the bank and less idea than
a mole where any more would come from for at least nine

more months, so I shopped very carefully. The most expensive item was the linoleum rugs. We found two exactly alike in a pretty rose-beige marble pattern which were less obnoxious than the garish flowers of the others, but they were also one dollar higher and I was in an agony of indecision about spending that extra dollar. Mr. G., reckless, thought I should shoot for the moon, so I did, but felt guilty all the way home.

We bought yellow paint for the woodwork and a heavy, oatmeal-textured building paper for the walls. It had a nice, soft, gray-blue color. It was also fifty-four inches wide, as all building paper is, but I thought less than nothing of that. I just liked the color and the texture and the unbelievable cheapness of it.

Mister G. eyed it dubiously. "Do you know how to paper?" he asked.

"No," I said, "but all the women on the ridge do their own papering. What they can do, we can do."

"We?" he raised an eyebrow.

"We," I said firmly.

It was no trick at all to lay the linoleums and if I do say so myself I wield a very dexterous paintbrush and the yellow woodwork was quite effective. But papering the walls was something else again.

We lacked every tool a professional paperer requires — scaffold, brushes, cutting knives and paste. We made a scaffold by balancing a long board on two kitchen chairs. We made lumpy homemade paste of flour and water. Our brushes were rags and our cutting knives were a pair of scissors and a blunt and nicked butcher knife. It had been blunted and nicked from cutting the cardboard cartons.

It was August and we had one day left before my mother arrived. We had two rooms to paper in that one day. We were up at daybreak to begin. In those years mornings were my best times. I was always full of energy and as chattery as a jaybird. Mister G. on the other hand is slow-motion in the morning and he requires a full hour of absolute silence and peace before admitting the day has begun. I thought nothing, therefore, of his sour look.

We moved along, finding the fifty-four inch paper unexpectedly hard to handle, but not impossible. We did the walls first and we soon developed a rhythm and routine and eventually Mister G. came out of his gloom and saved me from my running monologue. He began to speak, enough at least to answer me, and we worked so well together and so rapidly that the walls were finished by the middle of the morning. When we stopped then for coffee and cigarettes I boasted rather smugly that there was actually nothing to this wallpapering after all. "All we have left," I said, "is the ceilings."

Ringling Brothers circus tent wouldn't have seemed bigger before it was over! Nothing, absolutely nothing, would make a strip of that heavy paper, fifty-four inches wide and fifteen feet long, stay up. I can't think now why it didn't occur to us to cut it in two and work with narrower strips, all I know is it didn't and we pasted and sweated and trimmed and tried, again and again and again. I would stick an end to the ceiling. Mister G. would lift the strip and slowly walk the teetering scaffold to the opposite end while I scampered along behind trying frantically to smooth and brush and make it stick. As fast as he turned it loose, it sagged, drooped, and finally fell.

I have no idea how many times we repeated this without any success at all. We got hotter and hotter and sweatier and sweatier and madder and madder. Mister G. got very red in the face and ominously quiet. I didn't know it was the last time, but we cut one more strip and smeared the lumpy paste over it. Mister G. took his position with the strip lifted over his head. "When I start," he said, "begin swiping and for God's sake swipe fast!"

Grimly I determined that this time I would swipe so fast and so furiously the stuff wouldn't have a chance to pull loose. He hoisted the strip, placed it carefully, and began his slow walk along the scaffold. I followed, swiping desperately.

Halfway across, the end of the strip began to sag and buckle. I darted back and took a wild swipe at it, got it back up and stuck, but the middle had now started to sag. I scampered to it and wiped crazily and wildly, here, there, and everywhere. It was coming loose again, all over loose! My frantic scurryings were making the scaffold teeter precariously and Mister G. yelled a warning. Too late. A chair went over and the plank collapsed. I leaped to safety but Mister G. fell heavily and with desolation such as I have seldom felt I watched fifteen feet of building paper settle slowly over his head and drape him in a gluey winding sheet.

Nothing happened for a few solemn moments. Immobilized in paperer's paste and building paper and, for all I knew, with a broken leg, he just sat. I was transfixed myself, too horrified to move, too frightened to speak.

Then there came a stirring under the drapage, just a heave here and there, a sort of slow billowing. It was like a dreamy slow-motion scene from an old Laurel and Hardy film. After a time of heave and billow, two arms came out and strug-

glingly began to pull and pluck at the nauseous mess, degree
by infinitely slow degree freeing his head and hair, his face
and shoulders. When that much of him was free, Mister G.
lunged up and with fingers spread finickily plucked the rest
of the stuff from his shirt and bluejeans. He didn't say a word.
He didn't even look at me. Still very slowly he gathered up
the entire length of crumpled, sticky paper. He gathered and
gathered and wadded and wadded, and then he threw it just
as hard as he could throw it and just as far as he could
throw it.

I watched it rise, sail through the air, and settle fatefully
and inevitably glue-side down on what was left of breakfast
on the kitchen table. I had a hysterical impulse to giggle as
I thought of paperer's paste and butter, cold ham and eggs, to
say nothing of half a bowl of cream gravy, all mixed together.
I restrained it. This was no time to tempt fate!

Mister G. brushed himself off, washed his face and hands
and combed his hair. Then he stalked to the door, drew himself up and announced, roaringly, "*Never* ask me to help with
housework again!"

Which I thought most unfair. When did papering become
housework? But before I could roar back he was gone. And
he didn't come home until dark. By that time I had whittled
the building paper into squares and pasted it up, it stuck, and
all evidences of the storm, the high wind which had blown,
were nicely cleaned away. A good meal was also waiting.

This, too, Mister G. was doubtless telling his young friend.
Don't begin helping with the housework. Set your foot down
immediately. Don't get lassoed into wiping that first dish, or
scouring that first floor, or papering that first wall!

But perhaps the time Mister G. roared that has had the most

effect on our lives was when he flatfootedly refused to try to make water run uphill for me.

This was after we had bought what we called the "big farm." By any other standards than those of the Kentucky hills a hundred and six acres may be a very small farm but after our original forty it seemed quite expansive to us.

Some wag once quipped, and I'd be willing to bet it was a ridgerunner, that the only way to keep a woman happy is to keep her barefoot and pregnant. Unfortunately Mister G. could do neither with me. We were past the barefoot stage, with a little money to jingle in our jeans now, and since children had not made their appearance in the ten years of our marriage there was no good reason to suppose they ever would.

It was probably toward the end of the first year on the big farm that I began to look around me speculatively, ponder the bank account, and hanker anew for the two things I had had a yearning for most of my life, a log house and a body of water.

I was born with one foot in the past and a log house is to me the most beautiful structure man ever built. I never saw one that I didn't envy the owner and want to pick it up and bring it home with me. For years I had hoped that some day we could build one ourselves. The time seemed approaching.

I had also lived most of my life with some mystic love of water and a great longing to live beside it at work in me. Never had the circumstances of my life allowed me to gratify it. I grew up on a western prairie, lived most of my adult life in cities, and was now perched on one of the driest hilltops in Kentucky.

The sea was clearly out of the question, though I would have liked that best. A lake was also out of the question, and

I sensed that even a pond might be impossible. But if I was willing to settle for a brook flowing through the yard, just a little creek not more than a few feet wide, surely that could be managed.

I thought I knew what Mister G.'s reactions would be to either project, the house or the brook, and I had no difficulty deciding to begin with what seemed to me the simpler — the brook. I also determined to say nothing at all until I had worked it out myself and then I would present it to him, *fait accompli* as it were.

We lived on a long ridgesaddle where water is hard enough come by for household purposes. We had a deep drilled well that provided us with enough water for cooking and drinking but it couldn't even furnish us with a full water system in the house and we had to eke out with rainwater during the summer when the level fell very low. Obviously the well was going to be no great help with a brook.

A steep hollow fell away from the foot of the yard in front of the house and I kept thinking about a spring that was reportedly located on one of its slopes. If the spring had a good flow and if it didn't go dry in the summer it might, I thought, have possibilities. I clambered down one day and searched it out. There was a rock-lined pool now clogged with the leaf-fall of years, twigs and branches and other sediment, but flowing into it steadily down a mossgrown channel was a cold clear stream of water. It was certainly no gush but it was also more than a trickle. The spring itself was hidden under a ledge of rock. I cleared it all out and stood and surveyed it with excitement. This was better than I had hoped.

I questioned Mister G.'s mother about it. Yes, it was a good spring. In fact, when Felix Price first built the house the family had depended on the spring for all their water. They hadn't drilled the well for years. Sarah Price kept her milk and butter at the spring and did her washing down there. They packed water to the house for all other purposes. No, it never went dry. That was why the Prices had valued it so highly.

My glee was mounting daily now but I still said nothing. I traipsed down that hollow dozens of times eying the spring and the pool, deciding exactly where and how an electric pump could be installed. Then I went carefully over the yard looking for the most likely spot to build a pool to hold the water to be pumped up from the spring. I thought the highest place would be best. Running diagonally across the yard, following the natural slope, I could see the narrow, rock-bedded channel, where the overflow from the pool could race and form my brook. I went over and over and over it and when it was all clear to me and I had a logical, step-by-step spiel worked out, I approached Mister G. with enthusiasm.

I have rarely seen him more shaken.

He didn't even give me time to go into my spiel. At the very first mention of a brook and spring water pumped uphill he backed off and stared at me and thundered, "Have you completely lost your mind? No!"

And as was usual with him under stress, he stalked out of the house.

I never mentioned the brook again and of course I never did get around to mentioning the log house. Under the circumstances I thought it better not to.

But for some reason we sold the big farm the next year. And for some reason two years later we decided to buy a small place down in the valley. It was interesting, too, that right through the middle of this acreage, right through the middle of the yard in fact, a sparkling, clear, rushing little creek known as Spout Springs Branch made its way.

And for some reason the four-room farmhouse was not nearly big enough for us. And for some reason we just happened to own a log fishing camp on the river. And for some reason it wouldn't be a bit of trouble to move it. And buy another few sets of logs to add to it. And tear down the farmhouse. And build a lovely, charming, rambling old log house right under the sycamores on the banks of Spout Springs Branch.

And Mister G. didn't even think about roaring.

All I had to do was get him to town for a couple of years and let his dislike of towns work on him, pen him up in an apartment with his itch for a little piece of land all his own, and I got my brook, ready-made, and my log house, without a single apoplectic-rare-back-on-his-hind-legs-and-show-you-who's-boss-roar. He was too glad to get out in the open again.

I haven't heard him mention his theory that husbands have an easier time of it, wives are at least temporarily happier, and there is less sturm-und-drang all around if, within reason, wives are allowed to believe they have their own way, in a long time. Maybe he wanted a log house, too. Maybe he even wanted a creek.

Chapter 2
Unjolly Farmers

THERE WERE more practical reasons for selling the big farm
than my hankering for a creek though I am still of the opinion
there were none more valid. If you have had a strong life-
long yearning for a thing you'd better try at least once to
satisfy it. You may come a cropper but you'll at least get it
out of your system.

We should never have bought the farm in the first place.

I know *why* we did, of course. We meant to farm. But I
can't think why we thought we *needed* to farm, or *wanted*
to farm, or even *could* farm.

It is true Mister G. was born and reared on a ridge farm
only a mile from where we now lived. It was the kind of
little farm that barely supports breath in the body, and a
man and a horse, a hoe and a plow were the sum total of equipment. From the day he was old enough to be put to work

Mister G. had detested everything about the whole process of farming.

But he did love the country and by now I had become an enthusiastic convert to country living myself. Once the shortage of money had been taken care of and we could be comfortable both of us enjoyed it and didn't want to live permanently anywhere else. We liked a spread of space all around us; we liked being able to walk out over our own land; we loved birds and woods animals, the river, the hills. We liked not being hemmed in by too-near neighbors. We liked not only watching the turn of the seasons but breathing them and feeling them closely. What we wanted, without realizing it, was simply to live in the country and not live off it. We loved nature but we didn't want nature pushing us around. A small vegetable garden and a few flowers were all the plowing and planting we needed to say grace over.

Why it didn't occur to us to buy four or five acres and build a home and have what we really wanted is quite a mystery. But it didn't and instead we bought a hundred and six acres with every kind of mechanical and expensive equipment made for farming and set out to be farmers as well as writers. It nearly killed us both.

I can only suppose that living again in the community where he had been reared the ways of the community bore in very strongly on Mister G. And the ways of the community are that if you live in the country it is automatically for the purpose of farming. You don't just sit in the middle of several acres and enjoy them. You are supposed to work like fury from sunup to sundown plowing and planting, weeding and hoeing, mending fences, feeding and milking, and most important of all you're supposed to hold tobacco grow-

ing very nearly sacred. For a hundred and fifty years tobacco
has been the biggest cash crop of Kentucky farmers and it is
still an occupational disease with any man who has as much as
one tenth of an acre allotted to him by the government.

All of this was as much a part of Mister G. as his blood
and bones and I think he did a good job of convincing himself that his loathing of farming applied only to his boyhood
and the poor, rocky little acreage he had scrabbled over so
hard.

For whatever reason, as soon as there was enough money,
Mister G. wanted a real farm, with plenty of equipment, and
a chance to do some real farming. And I thought he knew
what he wanted. I didn't know the first thing about what we
were getting into. Blithely and with my usual ignorant optimism I went along with buying the big farm. Most of the
equipment came with it — tractor and plows and cultivators,
hay rakes, fertilizer spreaders, scoops and shovels and saws and
so forth. I even forgot something I have always believed —
that if the good Lord has seen fit to endow you with a set of
mental muscles that will earn a living for you, why do it with
those of your back? I have successfully avoided using my
back muscles most of my life, but they were sure due a work-
out when we acquired the farm.

I have great respect for the honest craftsman who enjoys
working with his hands, or the husbandman who truly loves
to till the soil and milk cows and slop pigs. I'm just not one
of them. But I didn't know it yet. There is a lot of the ham
in me and for a while, as usual, I was able to slip into the role,
the role for the time being acting like a farmer's wife.

Nothing I ever did in my entire life filled me with such
dreadful, dreary, deadly, monotonous, killing boredom.

Though I tried I was never able to have any communication with cows. All they do is glare at you balefully from their huge bovine eyes and chew their cud at you, switch their tails craftily in your face and step on you if you give them half a chance. I never saw one that acted the least bit friendly toward me and I always approached them with a weather eye on the nearest fence post. I wanted a safe perch if I had to retreat in a hurry. The few times I tried to learn to milk were highly unsuccessful. The cows not only refused to cooperate, they were actively unfriendly. It was with great relief I learned eventually that Mister G. did not expect the farmer's wife to help with the milking.

I got no more response from any of the rest of the stock on the place. Pigs just grunt and plow up the ground with their snoots and they'd just as soon kill you as not if you get in their way when they're stampeding for the feeding trough. Mister G. made friends with the sow, who used to rub up against him and let him scratch her ears, but every time I looked at her I remembered we had had to separate her from her litter to keep her from eating the runts.

But I do believe the least responsive thing the Lord ever made is a chicken. I don't honestly think he meant to make them. His hand just slipped and we've been stuck with them ever since. They don't even know enough to come in out of the rain and will trail a flock of babies around in a downpour until the last one of them is drowned if you don't watch them. And the things a chicken will eat are enough to turn the stoutest stomach against country eggs or fried country chicken.

The truth is that not since the first man pushed a pointed stick around in some dirt and planted a handful of seeds have there been sadder or unhappier farmers than Mister G. and

I were. And we persisted in this insanity for three long years.

We had some beef cattle, though not many, a few calves, some milk cows, some pigs, a flock of chickens and three dogs. We committed ourselves early to babysitting livestock and for at least two of the three years we doggedly and obstinately pursued this uninspired occupation. It was as though having committed ourselves to all this plowing and planting and dancing attendance on animals there was no alternative.

I consider those three years of our lives a vast wasteland, the stupidest thing we ever did. They managed to gray Mister G.'s hair, thin him down to the flatness of a razor strap, give him a muscle-pinched back and make permanent an arthritic condition in his knees.

They stunted what creative ability I have and because I was too bone-tired most of the time to think, much less write, they made what had been such a joy to me just one more dreary chore through which I had to drag myself. And they turned my stomach forever against anything homegrown except vegetables. To this day I can't think of country milk and cream and butter and eggs without shuddering. That man who goes into ecstasies over such things is usually, I have found, a good safe distance from having to produce them. He is merely nostalgic about them and the taste he remembers is usually a child's uncritical taste.

One week of watching what our country chickens ate on the range was enough to convince me that neither they nor their eggs were fit for consumption. We proceeded to sell the eggs and chickens and bought eggs from caged-layer coops where the food was controlled, and bought chickens to fry from brooder houses.

And I have only to remember those endless gallons of warm,

foaming milk Mister G. brought to the house for me to take care of to find it almost impossible to drink even homogenized milk.

I made butter faithfully. But the rest of the day I churned my stomach was uneasy. You make country butter by skimming the cream off milk for days. When there is perhaps a gallon of it you set it out of the refrigerator to turn. This means it must reach a precise stage of age and souring. The smell is very much like that of a sewer. Then you churn it and that does nothing to improve the odor. Day-fresh butter? There isn't any such thing. There is only week-old cream battered into solid form.

Eventually we reached the stage of being flooded with milk. At that time neither the Pet nor Carnation Milk Companies ran milk routes our way as they do today, buying whole milk. A cream truck passed twice a week but the cream station in town was interested only in cream, naturally. When we came to the place of running the risk of being drowned in milk even after feeding it to everything on the place that would drink it, Mister G. decided we must buy a cream separator and sell cream. The "blue john" left, he said, we could then pour out.

That was the day! Have you any idea how many parts a cream separator has? At least ten thousand, all of them small, all of them peculiarly shaped, all of them precision made, and all of them fitting together into unalterable positions, all of them requiring washing and sterilizing twice a day. Talk about slavery! If separating cream is any part of your life you'd be better off in the salt mines.

Those ten thousand separator parts caused our friend, old Sud Pigeon, to come to grief one day and his cream separator to come to a violent end.

Old Sud was a sucker and a soft sell. A peddler selling anything from salve to linoleum rugs to house paint found a sure sale at Sud's place. He had a solid income from various kinds of "draws." He was a canny old man and knew how to get on any kind of county, state, or federal welfare list. I never knew him to do a lick of work. Somebody else always worked for Sud, and one way or another he usually had a little cash money in his jeans and was easily separated from it.

The more bright and shining an article was, the more chrome it had on it, the more enamored Sud would be of it and the more determined he would be to buy it. He bought a vacuum cleaner one time. There wasn't a rug in his house, or a piece of upholstered furniture. There wasn't even a curtain at the windows. But that vacuum cleaner was a pretty thing, all glisteny and bright, so he bought it. And he bought an electric washing machine before rural electrification was even a dream. He set both these gadgets on his front porch for the whole world to see. Useless and expensive and bought on the installment plan as they were, they gave him, in his own eyes, status in the community. It didn't matter to Sud that he couldn't use them. He owned them and there they sat, proving that Sud Pigeon was a step ahead of everybody else in the community.

When a produce house in one of the nearby towns started a cream route down the ridge it wasn't long until cream separator salesmen made their appearance. There is a regular racket of peddling to country people and the operators have a sensitive nose for any new developments. They swarm over an area like squawking starlings, sell inferior goods and pick the pockets of naive and unwary farmers.

Electricity had come to our parts by this time so the first

peddler hauling a cream separator around in the back of his battered truck made a quick sale to Sud. And he went about as proud as a peacock telling everybody who would listen that he was going to get rich selling cream. This contraption he had just bought squeezed the last drop of cream from the milk and all you had to do was pour it in a can and set it by the side of the road where the cream truck would pick it up. A few days later you got a check, a magnificent check naturally.

I'm not sure anyone tried to discourage him though somebody did remind him he had only one measly, muley cow and how could he get rich off her? It made no difference. When Sud bought a new gadget he had total faith in it. That cream separator, not his cow, was going to make him rich.

Sud's wife — his third, incidentally — could read but she hardly ever troubled to. Her eyes were bad, she said, and it gave her a headache to ponder words. Besides they hardly ever made any sense. So when the cream separator was delivered it was entirely in keeping with her philosophy that she should completely ignore the book of instructions that accompanied it. Helter-skelter, hit or miss, she threw all those innumerable parts in the hopper, Sud standing by with his hand on the switch barely able to control his eagerness to see the contraption in operation.

We didn't see what happened but their sixteen-year-old boy, Red, told us about it the next day. "The agent, he left it ready to use," he said, "but Mag let Johnnie play with it to keep him quiet and Willie Bob, he wanted to see all them parts, too." (Johnnie was the baby, some four years old, and Willie Bob was a grown son not all there mentally.)

"Between 'em," Red said, "they taken it apart and got them pieces scattered around considerably.

"Pa went to milk and he told Mag to collect up the pieces and git 'em all put together. They was a book come with it with some pictures how to put it together but Mag said it wouldn't make no sense to her, she'd just put 'em in the best way she could. Said they'd all come outen the contraption and they was bound to go back in. We collected up all the parts we could find and she poked 'em in whichaway.

"We got 'em all in one way or another and Pa come in with the milk. He was real excited and in the worst way to see the contraption work. He poured the milk in and said, 'Now, I'll turn the switch on and we'll see some cream come out that spout.'

"He done so, but he mortally did step back in a hurry. You never heard nothing but a thrashing machine make more noise than that contraption done! It commenced growling and grinding and clattering and bucking like it aimed to walk right out the door! Sounded just like it was chewing its insides up!

"Next thing we knowed milk was spouting clean to the ceiling and we all commenced ducking and then the part that held the milk come loose and flew off and sailed plumb through the window. Broke the windowpane and taken the frame with it.

"Then seemed like all hell broke loose and all them little bitty pieces commenced flying in ever' direction and they wasn't no way to duck 'em all. Mag got conked on the side of the head with one and if Pa'd had e'er tooth in his head hit'd been knocked out for he had his mouth open squalling at us to git outside, git out on the porch, git away 'fore we all got killed. Said the dad-blamed thing had went crazy and was aiming to maim us all.

"I seen one of them little screw pieces fly straight in his mouth. His eyes kind of popped and he said he b'lieved he'd swallered it but it likely wouldn't kill him it was so little.

"We all made it out on the porch finally and kept watch through the door. Pa was real put out. Said he hadn't never seen nothing go flinging its parts around like that 'thout no call for it and he didn't aim to stand for it. Said it was just plumb dangerous to have such a thing in the house. Which it was.

"When it got quietened down finally he got up the nerve to stick his head in. Didn't nothing happen so he said he reckoned it had belched up all the innards it had and was satisfied now.

"Mag said not to expect her to make no use of such a fool thing no more and Pa said warn't nobody going to make use of it. Said he aimed for the peddler to pick it up quick as he could git a holt of him and he aimed to git his down payment back. Said he'd been told a lie and what he ort to do was set the law on that peddler and sue him. Said one of us could of been killed. Which we could of." Red scratched his head ruefully. "Hit was shore a narrer excape."

Which it was.

Our cream separator never did belch up its innards but it took a daily toll of time and energy as long as we persisted in our folly.

I think it was the first week in May that year when an unprecedented norther blew in on us, sent the thermometer down to a shivering eight above zero, frostbit the entire vegetable garden and the tobacco plant bed, and froze Mister G.'s ears when he tried to milk that morning.

Like his father, Mister G. is an unhurried man and I rarely saw him move except at his own leisurely pace. But frozen ears brought him in a dead run to the house, with clattering, empty milk pails. "I'll be damned," he roared, "if we're going to live this way any longer! We're going to sell every blasted head of stock on the place, rent the land, and live like human beings again!"

Sweeter words were never spoken! I was dreadfully afraid he might change his mind when the sun came out, but he had had it. He meant it. He was through.

One of the happiest days I can remember was that on which trucks carried away every head of beef, every calf, every milk cow, every pig, to market. We didn't even try to sell the chickens. We just gave them away. And when the last thing possessing hide or feathers was gone, we went a little crazy. We packed a bag and headed for the city for a week-end of delirious freedom. It was glorious and jubilant and hilarious — the first time both of us had been off the place together for three years. It was the celebration of our lives.

When we returned Mister G. set to work to find a renter for the land. I saw no reason why we shouldn't just let it go back to weeds and sprouts but he was horrified at the idea. You didn't, it seemed, let cleared land revert.

"Why not?" I asked. "It might improve the national economy if a great many farmers turned their land over to weeds and sprouts for a generation or two. Maybe the whole country would be better off if more farmers would just quit. Might take care of surpluses and soil conservation and reforestation."

"And increase unemployment," he growled. "Where would they go?"

We then got into a lofty argument about the place of the

small family farm in American life today, the problem of migration movements, transference of cultures, social welfare and even unwed mothers.

Since Mister G. obviously was not going to let our acres revert to weeds and sprouts or even be planted in seedling pines, I prayed he would find a renter. He did. A cousin of his, of which he has hundreds, wanted for some insane reason to work more land. Well, bully for him! He could sure work our hundred and six acres with absolutely no interference from me.

One good thing seems to lead to another, or perhaps it's that one positive action leads to the next one. It was less than a week after renting the land that Mister G. came home from Campbellsville with a grin spreading from ear to ear. He could go to work on the *News-Journal*, the Campbellsville weekly newspaper, if he so wanted, and he did so want.

Mister G. had had a smattering of journalism in school, but more than that we had talked all around the edges of some day putting out a very small, perhaps monthly, or even semi-occasionally, country newspaper ourselves. In the Arkansas Ozarks we had come across two such country presses, both one-man operations, and both fairly successful if you didn't expect too much. The old hand-set type and manual presses had fascinated us. If we ever did this ourselves, however, Mister G. would need to know all he could learn about the mechanics. This was his perfect opportunity. We have never, of course, felt we could afford this plunge, but we still have a fondness for the idea and when we begin to draw Social Security we may get around to putting it into effect.

For three months Mister G. commuted. Campbellsville

was only twenty miles from our front door and the distance, in the summer, was nothing. Happily I wrote all day every day (that was the year *Hannah Fowler* was written) but quit in time to have a good meal ready when Mister G. drove up. Each busy with engrossing work, each possessed of a grand sense of freedom, it was the most joyous and productive summer we had had in many years.

In late August, however, we suddenly woke up to certain facts. We lived on a rural road which was far from an all-weather road. The winter rains and freezes would play havoc with it. Mister G. might, on some days, not be able to drive over it, or he might be marooned in town, unable to get home. There was no telephone service to the ridge. We had lightly dismissed my isolation during the summer, but winter was a very different thing. All sorts of unpleasant things could happen during the long, cold, dark months. We pondered and we reached a decision. We would take an apartment in town to use five days a week. On weekends we would come home. It became my job to find the apartment.

I take no delight in suburbia. If I'm going to live in town I want to live in town where I can conveniently reach everything I need on my own two feet. Years of city living had taught me this is not only less wearing and tearing but less expensive in the long run. If you're going to live far enough out to need transportation you might as well go the whole hog and live in the open country. So my search was confined to the area nearest the town's business district.

I finally found a spacious apartment over one of the business buildings on one of the busiest streets in Campbellsville. It was in appalling condition and when Mister G. saw it he wasn't at all impressed. But I liked it. The living room was huge, twenty by thirty feet with eleven-foot ceilings no less. It was also at the rear and no street noises could be heard. I knew it would make an ideal place for me to work. There was a bedroom with lovely closet space, a dining room, an entrance hall, a tiny kitchen and bath. We took it and when it had been cleaned and painted and refurbished it became a comfortable and elegant and beautiful place to live. I wrote *The Believers* that winter in that grand ballroom of a living room and not even the country had given me more quiet and isolation. It was a wonderful workroom.

For perhaps a month we did go home for the weekends but a young married couple, the husband just returned from Korea, were having a difficult time finding a place to live. They asked to rent the farmhouse and, feeling sympathy for them and selfish at keeping it empty all week, we let them have it.

We now became town dwellers entirely and this, perhaps, paved the way and made it easier when the time came to sell.

It came shortly and quite unexpectedly. The same cousin who was renting the land came to see us one Saturday night and proposed to buy the farm. It was hard to believe our ears. We had all too much money tied up in it and we had never expected to get out from under that grisly white elephant. But here was a man seriously proposing to take it off our hands, at a price that would repay our original investment plus most of the improvements we had made, and what was most astonishing of all to us, he had a fistful of nice cold cash with which to pay. It was too good to be true!

Quickly, lest he vanish and it prove only a happy dream, I looked at Mister G. and he looked at me and we grinned and shouted with one voice, "Sold!" We were finally, positively, and forever through with a farm.

Two years later we bought this one at Spout Springs!

Chapter 3
The Place Called Home

But we *had* learned some things.

For one thing, never again would cows, calves, chickens and pigs sap our energy and time. We have religiously stuck to this although Mister G. gets a wistful look in his eyes occasionally when he sees a beautiful milk cow or new-born calf or an unusually well-proportioned White Leghorn hen. The country in a boy dies hard. I nudge him and whisper "May Day."

The universal distress signal is enough to recall his own distresses when he had cows and chickens. The decision to get rid of them was wholly his. He can have them again if he pleases, but not without warning.

And though we had to buy more land than we wanted or needed, it is still only a little farm, just a postage-stamp place of fourteen valley acres and fifty-six acres of woodland up the hollow. The timber requires no care or attention from us. It just sits up there on the hillside and grows. The valley acres we promptly planted in grass which also just sits there and grows. No sweat — so it wasn't as mad as it sounds.

After twelve years of marriage which included very mixed experiences — city jobs, writing, farming and newspapering — we had come finally to a time and place of knowledge, of ourselves, of our needs and wants.

Our needs and wants were relatively simple. We were writers, first, last and always. Mister G. was branching into more and more journalism and I had become by now an old professional in the field of historical fiction. Our need was uninterrupted time and rather solitary living. The country did, after all, offer it best.

That squared, fortunately, with our wants. I suppose we were never anything but temporary town dwellers at heart. We were lucky enough to be able to afford what we needed and wanted. We wanted now a few acres and we wanted to build the home we had so long envisioned.

We joyously and willingly restricted ourselves in our search for a place to Adair County. It had to be Adair County and it had, further, to be in the north end of Adair County, fenced by the hills of home and Green River, that stream about which we feel so possessive and which we love so dearly.

My good friend Eloise Baerg, of Fayetteville, Arkansas, visited me briefly one time. She was struck, amused, and a little awed, by the emphasis Kentuckians put on county divisions. She had not encountered it before.

My own reactions of twenty-three years before when I came to Kentucky first were recalled. I had so long forgotten them, had become myself so accustomed to the Kentucky emphasis, that those reactions were sunk almost beyond dredging up and I found myself startled by Eloise's astonishment. Like a native I now place people or events by their counties.

It has come about over the years that many strangers find their way to our doors to meet us, to interview us, to have books autographed, or just to say a warm and friendly word. They identify themselves by name and then by city and state — Colorado, California, Kansas, Minnesota, New Jersey, and so on. Kentuckians do this differently. We are first and foremost from Metcalfe County, or Hart County, or Lincoln County, or Fayette County, or, by golly, from Adair County. Only after we have mentioned the county do we mention the city or town. On hearing the county name any Kentuckian can immediately pigeonhole another Kentuckian. Each section of the state, each county, has its own peculiar characteristics (at least to us), its own traits and differentnesses, and its own history which has given them to it. We know that a man from Adair County is no more like a man from one of the mountain counties or the bluegrass counties or the northern counties than a mule is like a horse. There is a surface resemblance and there are enough similarities for a meeting of minds, but the attitudes, the frame of reference, even the speech of a man from another county will be not quite like ours. Just as when traveling across the United States each state will have something peculiarly its own, a special look and flavor, to us there is a differentness and distinction between counties.

My daughter's father-in-law, for instance, says even the *air* in Shelby County is different, smells sweeter, is lighter and freer. To him Shelby County is obviously the paradise Daniel Boone was talking about when he said heaven must be a Kentucky sort of place.

There is something touching in the fierceness with which each Kentuckian feels that same thing about his own county. There are one hundred and twenty counties in Kentucky, almost twice as many as in New York state, and in each one its proud native sons look a little down their noses at the other hundred and nineteen. We do too. They can't be as good as ours.

But within the county there is inevitably that native place, that heartland, that is really home. For us it is that sweet strip of ridge and valley bordering Green River, both narrow and short. It begins at Dunbar Hill on the west and ends at Old Neatsville on the east. It is barely three miles long, never more than a mile wide and in places it crowds to within a quarter of a mile of the river.

We have a passion for Green River that amounts to almost a mania. But we have always had sense enough to know that you don't love a whole river, for a river changes its personality with every mile. You love a little piece of a river, that little piece you've fished over for years, swum in, boated on, and watched in all its seasonal changes. You love that little piece you know as well as you know the inside of your home; it is, in fact, your larger home, every riffle and deep, every shoal and pool, every bend and twist, possessed of sweet familiarity.

Actually we would have liked to build on the river itself and there was one location we coveted very much. Somebody had built a fishing camp overlooking a stretch of noisy beautiful fast water and we walked around and about it, dreaming, for days. It was a sweet and likely place, built on a shelf that was high enough to be safe from all but the biggest tides. But it wasn't for us. Three men owned the building but they did not own the land on which it stood. The land was tied up in the settlement of an estate.

We never came across another such likely building site on the river so regretfully we had to back up into the valley.

We never did, in fact, come across any likely building site with only a few acres. Nobody wanted to part with two or three acres because under the tobacco allotment law if even so much as one acre of a farm is sold a tiny percentage of the tobacco allotment must go with it. Naturally nobody in his right mind would part with even a tenth of one percent of his tobacco allotment.

We were in no great hurry and we kept patient. We just drove and explored and questioned. At one time we were within inches of buying the Spout Springs Schoolhouse. Mister G.'s uncle had bid it in at the auction held when the county schools were consolidated and the one-room schools abandoned. It was a good, sturdy, fairly new building and he had made it into a sound four-room cottage. We examined it and thought we needn't do much but add several log rooms and put in a plumbing system and we would have precisely what we wanted. One acre of land, just enough for a lawn, went with it. So certain was Mister G.'s uncle that he wanted to sell that he accepted a check from us for a down payment, balance to be paid on transfer of the deed.

Mister G.'s uncle had for years harbored a great longing to move to the post-office village, Knifley. Optimistically he had agreed to sell to us — "made a trade" as the saying goes around here. But he ran into unexpected trouble finding a house to buy in the village and much to his embarrassment and chagrin he had to back out of his trade with us. You just don't do that here. If you give your word, you stick to it, and to be a man of your word means everything in our area. But Lee had no alternative. Obviously he couldn't sell us the schoolhouse-cottage if he couldn't find a place to move into. But no man was ever more put out or red-faced than he was when we came to pick up the deed and give him our check for the balance of his price. His wife (young and second) told us he had offered her ten dollars to take the blame on herself — if she would say she had changed her mind about selling. We couldn't have believed it anyhow for Bonnie, more than anybody, wanted to get her young children into town where they wouldn't have to wade Spout Springs Branch to catch the school bus.

We now own the schoolhouse but it came to us differently.

That day we felt pretty downhearted when we drove away. We had been pleased and happy to find, at last, the single acre we wanted and the good, solid building to form a core for a home, and the beautiful everlasting spring on the hillside above that would furnish a water system with a minimum of effort. And there was the brook, or branch as it is called here, which cut near the corner of the house. Speaking for myself because Mister G. just gloomed, I felt it very

unjust to be denied when our hopes had been so high — not
that I blamed Lee, just fate.

I needn't have worried.

Edsel Spires, whose small farm adjoined, was waiting at
the gate for us. He was already privy to Lee's defection,
of course. He and his wife had talked it over and they
had decided to see if we might be interested in their place.
When he saw our car turn up the lane to the schoolhouse
he stationed himself to wait for our return, knowing what
we would learn at Lee's. Would we be interested? Would
we look at the place? Would we consider it?

It was a bigger place than we wanted but it never hurts
to look, so we looked.

You come down into this valley over Dunbar Hill on the
west by a winding road which, until a few years ago, was
narrow and very sparsely graveled.

In the old days the state was not building rural roads and
Green River farmers had no way to transport their tobacco
and corn to market except over the ancient wagon roads
which were mud-clogged in winter and dust-fogged in
summer.

Mr. Ray Williams, Mr. Cassius Breeding, Mr. Joe Green
Knifley, Mr. Gus Dunbar, and others, pooled their resources
and equipment and built a road from the old Green River
bridge to Knifley, some eight miles in all. To pay themselves back they charged a toll for traveling, twenty-five
cents for a four-wheeled vehicle and team, five cents for a
pedestrian. There were two tollgates between the bridge
and the village.

When he was a boy, Mister G. walked that road to Knifley
many times but he never paid a toll. He took to the woods

just before reaching the gate, bypassed it and returned to the road on the other side.

When the road had paid back their original investment and made them a little profit the valley farmers turned it over to the state. Mister Ray, who is now in his eighties, tells me it was never again kept in such good condition as it was by the eight farmers who built it. That may be nostalgia talking, an old man remembering the days when his stint at road work came due, when he took out his tractor and graded and weeded and spread the thin layer of top gravel — and was younger and happier to be doing it. I think he might still like to be taking his turn, for old men's memories are very long.

When I first came over the road eighteen years ago with my new husband of less than a fortnight, it had been ten years since it was a toll road. To my unaccustomed eyes and bones it was a rough, corduroyed, muddy byroad. I did not realize that had it not been for the old roadbed of river gravel, solid and sturdy and hard, the ancient car which carried us would have bogged in mud before we had gone a mile.

Those farmers built exceedingly well. When the state decided, a few years ago, to blacktop the road, they followed, with remarkably few changes, the course of the old toll road and most of the changes they made were in the grade up the steep escarpment known as Dunbar's Hill.

You must drive over this steep and scenic escarpment to reach our valley. Then you drop swiftly, though meanderingly, down. The tumbled and rugged hills crowd you on the left hand, marching to the very verge of the road. On the right, the narrow valley spreads flatly to the river which

is marked by its line of trees. On the other side of the river
the hills rise sharply again.

These hills all about us are so roughly tumbled that a
stranger could find no beginning or end to them and even
men born here have been known to become lost in them.
When Mister G. attempted to survey the timberland belong-
ing to our little farm he became completely confused. And
he is no amateur surveyor. Also he was born not a mile
from where our timber tops out on Grace Ridge and man
and boy had hunted over every square foot of it. But he
couldn't survey it and lay it out.

The hills are so broken that a contour map shows whorls
like individual fingerprints, hundreds of them laid and over-
laid, creased and rumpled by the gashed ravines and hollows
down which the hundreds of small streams flow toward their
meeting with the river.

Near the head of the valley, a mile and a half perhaps
from the foot of Dunbar Hill, one of the longest of these
streams cuts down Sugar Camp Hollow. Spout Springs
Branch, with a watershed of three of the steepest miles in
the country, rises, strangely, in a dimpled indentation on
our old ridge farm.

On its banks stood the white frame farmhouse of Edsel
and Violet Spires which we had now to consider as the
place for our home.

Their price, we thought, when we had walked over the
land and looked at the house, was too high and we didn't
want the timberland. We wanted only the fourteen acres
around the house. They wouldn't consider selling any part
without the whole. Take it or leave it.

We decided to leave it and we did leave it for several days.

When we saw them next, they were in a mood to compromise and we were in a mood to compromise. We raised our offer a little bit and agreed to take the timber; they lowered theirs a little and we had a meeting of minds and before you could say Jack Robinson we owned a little piece of Spout Springs Branch, fourteen acres of valley land and fifty-six acres of timber.

And finally, and best of all, I had my creek flowing right through the yard. In fact, its near bank marks the limit of what we must mow each summer. Across it, and you cross only by hopping fleetfootedly from stone to stone, is the pasture and tobacco patch. Oh, yes, we had to take a tobacco allotment.

It is a pretty stream, as clear as crystal and icy cold. When we were building our log house my artist friend, Pansy Phillips, came one day to see what progress was being made. It was March, but the sun was bright and the thermometer stood at a warm and unusual eighty degrees. Pansy was hot. "I'm going to wade the creek," she said, shucking off her shoes and stockings. She dipped one toe in and yelped and hurried back into her shoes and stockings. The water was frigid. It is always cold, even in August, because it is spring fed and even the hottest sun warms it very little.

After the branch flows past our house, where it churns into white water often, it widens and gentles. It channels through a culvert under the road and then, wholly tamed, spreads itself placidly into a soft oozing slough which falls slightly to the river.

I have used this branch in many books, *The Enduring Hills,* *Miss Willie,* and others, but perhaps most notably in *Land Beyond the Mountains* where my imagination harnessed it to a mill wheel, dammed it to make a millpond in which tragedy occurred. I never weary of it and I count it one of the blessings of my life that any hour of the day I can look out the windows and watch its waters race by.

Here near the mouth of Spout Springs Branch, nine families have their homes and form the tiny settlement of Spout Springs. We have no post office nor any business section. Our mail comes by rural route from the village, six miles west of us, called Knifley. The nearest stores are those of Leland Grant and Buck Watson a mile and an eighth from us at the crossroads — all that is left of the once thriving community of Old Neatsville. We are a community only because we are a cluster of houses.

Our name derives from the great gushing spring on the hillside just up the hollow. Here, in the old days, a log schoolhouse was built. Inevitably it was called the Spout Springs School. The log building gave way to one of weathered frame which, in turn, gave way to a larger and better frame building painted white. Mister G.'s great-grandfather went to school in the log schoolhouse. His grandfather and father and he himself were housed in the first frame building. His younger brothers and sisters attended the "new" school. But they all went through eight grades in Spout Springs School.

Eventually Mister G.'s uncle, Lee Giles, found the house he wanted in Knifley and the schoolhouse changed hands, coming finally, long after our need for it had passed, into our hands. We felt sentimental about it, it adjoined our place, so we bought it. Occasionally we rent it, furnished scantily, for the summer, but mostly it stands there, a mute memorial to some mighty fine schooling.

We had come, now, full circle and home, and in the last warm days of August in the summer of 1957 we began to draw up tentative plans for the house we meant to build and to look about us for the sets of old logs we would need.

Chapter 4
By Guess and By God

THERE ARE still those who would tell you our house got built by guess and by God.

Not so. Oh, we did a lot of guessing — of the wrong kind all too often — and there was certainly one stage when the hand of Providence was clearly evident, but it wasn't luck that put this house together, though we could have used more of it.

There *was* a plan, a blueprint of sorts, changed and shifted so often that by the time we finished it was smudged and spotted beyond recognition; there was my blithe optimism and vast ignorance and bullheaded obstinacy; there was Mister G.'s ingenuity and commonsense understanding of engineering; and on the part of two neighbors who did much of the actual building there was a good-humored acceptance of our queer ideas, plus great native skill. I think they thought if we were crazy enough to throw our money away building a rambling old log house they might as well salvage a little of it for us by building as good a house as could be built.

It's true I did have a crawly feeling we might be bucking fate when one disastrous thing after another kept occurring, when we had to defy not only every sound theory of building time and time again but eventually the law of gravity itself; but by that time it was too late.

I do think Mister G. might have warned me beforehand that there isn't a square foot in the valley that's really land. It looks like land, feels like it, smells like it, and if you don't plow too deep plows like it, but it isn't land at all. It's tundra. It isn't quite the quivery kind they have in Alaska that trembles and shakes under every footstep but it's a kissing cousin to it. Only sixteen inches beneath the topsoil lies water and gravel. Either he wanted me to learn once and for all that there were some things about which I could not say let it come to pass and it would come to pass or he gave me credit for enough sense to look at the branch and know the water table lay exactly level with its bed. The only way I looked at the branch was with love and until he began to lay the plumbing pipes I had never heard of a water table!

However, once you start building a house you've committed yourself. You can't, when the chips are down, cry a pox on both your houses and walk away. There's nothing to do but survey your watery location with what sweetness of soul you can dredge up, pour good money after bad, grit your teeth, sweat a little harder, wipe away the tears of vexation and, at times, of despair, pick yourself up, brush yourself off and bull your way forward.

I was either blessed or cursed with a rubber-ball bounce of resiliency. Nothing gets me down permanently. I despair just as well and probably as often as the next person but in less time than most I bounce back, ready for the fray again, ready, even eager, to be up and at'em once more.

Besides, I'm not my mother's daughter for nothing. She had no use for weaklings and leaners and she reared her children on pungent jabs calculated to make them self-reliant. I grew up on her needling. Stand on your own two feet. Figure it out for yourself. Don't come to *me* with your problems. You got yourself into this mess, now get yourself out of it. *Can't* never got to the top of the hill. You'll never learn if you don't try. Second-best isn't good enough. Finish what you start. More backbone than wishbone is the secret of success. And always and forever, daily and almost hourly, she hammered into us "where there's a will there's a way." She never doubted that God and Lucy McGraw had given us the will, but she didn't mean for herself *or* God to find us the way. We had to do that for ourselves.

My mother had need of her own backbone in those days. She was eighteen (that seems to be the marrying year in our family — my grandmother, mother, myself and my daughter all married at eighteen) when she married my father, John Holt. A year later, at the turn of the century, she went with him from western Arkansas into the rough, tough frontier country of the Indian Territory.

She was one of several pretty, tender, sheltered daughters of a big, happy, comfortably off family. She was an accomplished musician, as were all the daughters, and she had a lovely contralto voice. She was also, even at that tender age, a graduate of the old Hiram and Lydia Institute. When I think of the subjects she had studied since the day she started to school it makes today's curricula seem pale and childish. Imagine eight years of Latin, and four years of German, and endless years of mathematics and history and English, rhetoric and literature, music, drama, art, to say nothing of something called "manners."

She was also mischievous, possessed of high spirits and a quick temper, a gift for laughing easily, and absolute courage and gallantry. She went from the comfort and gentleness in which she had been reared into a rugged coal camp as the wife of a very poor schoolteacher and she went with a high heart and complete gaiety. She never lost either.

I have heard her tell how she and my father made their furniture from boxes and crates and painted it themselves and how, lacking a rug for her best room, she stitched up yards of checked gingham and tacked it over fresh straw. She then hung curtains of the same checked gingham at her windows and in a day when doing-it-yourself was nothing to be proud of took immense pride in her own ingenuity.

To tell the truth my father and mother never did put too much emphasis on home furnishings. Our home was always a little skimpily and raggedly put together. The essentials were comfortable beds and chairs, a good lamp or two, a stove that would cook the meals, and rugs and curtains and fancy doodads just didn't matter. To this good day my mother doesn't have a complete set of dishes and if she ever had one I don't remember it, and she has the zaniest collection of odds and ends she calls furniture anybody ever saw. It couldn't matter less to her. Money, all her life, was better spent on books and music, travel and having fun than in any other way. Besides, housekeeping bored her. She was the world's best homemaker, for it was warm and radiant with love, but she was also the world's poorest housekeeper.

How she loved for my father to come in from school and say, "Lucy, let's go for a ride." How quickly she could shove a kettle of preserves to the back of the stove, step into her riding habit, and go for a long gallop over the prairie. And how little it bothered her to leave beds unmade, dishes unwashed, clothes unironed, and gather at a moment's notice all the things we needed for an overnight camp to fish. "Pooh," she'd say, "they'll wait. This chance to fish won't."

I have heard Lucy McGraw tell of her early years in the Indian Territory and I don't recall ever having heard her tell of hardships. "What hardships?" she would say. "There weren't any. Of course we were poor but so was everybody else. It was a poor country. But we had each other and we had you children and we had a grand good time and that made us rich. There were some worrisome times," she admitted under pressure. "When we lost our first baby, and when Janice had typhoid fever, and when I had peritonitis. Nobody escapes a few worries. But in the main we had a good, fine life."

It was what they made it.

And yet . . . and yet, when she first went to the Indian Territory it was still thought of as a lawless place, a robber's roost sort of place, and in that first little coal camp her neighbors were miners, most of them foreign-born with heavily accented English if they had any at all; and Choctaw Indians some of whom neither spoke nor understood English. But the things Lucy told about Dow, Indian Territory, nearly all concerned the good friendships and the fun, especially the friendship begun then that lasted a lifetime with John Snodgrass and his young wife, Annabelle. He was manager of the Company store, and the four young people shared a mutual love of fishing, camping, hunting, making music and dancing together.

Even the time the Union came to the mines with violence and bloodshed was invested with laughter. An attempt was made to dynamite the mine superintendent's home. "Your father," she told us (this was all before any of us were born) "ordered me to stay in the house with the doors locked."

"Did you?"

"Certainly not. That poor man's wife was scared out of her wits! She needed us. Annabelle and I marched right over there and took charge. We put her to bed and we cleaned up the mess and we cooked a good hot meal. When we left she had hold of herself again. Hide behind locked doors? How foolish!"

"Weren't you afraid?"

"Afraid of what? A few miners? Of course not. They weren't going to harm two women."

"But they tried to dynamite . . ."

"And that was wrong of them, and perhaps the best way to show them how wrong was for two women to walk right through their lines on an errand of mercy. The idea . . . putting dynamite under the superintendent's front porch. They might have killed somebody and I told them so. They should have been ashamed. As if the superintendent made Company policy. As if he didn't have his job to do the same as they had theirs. Their quarrel, I told them, was with the operators. Take it up with the owners, I said, and don't go around scaring women and children!"

"What did they do?"

"Nothing. Hung their heads and let us through."

"What happened next?"

"Oh, they got their union and it promptly priced the small operators right out of existence and most of those little coal towns became ghost towns. There isn't any permanent answer to the ills of humanity. The unions promised the millennium to the miners, but it hasn't come yet."

Well, some of that was later wisdom.

After two or three moves from one coal camp to another my parents settled finally in the small town of Kinta which was not in coal country. It lay on the edge of the prairie and was farming and ranching country and it was in the heart of the Choctaw nation. The Choctaw capital was only three miles away and had the nice French name of Sans Bois — we called it "San-boy." My first memories are of Kinta, but by that time the Indian Territory had become the state of Oklahoma and there was no longer any need of a Choctaw capital.

I have heard Lucy tell, also, of the tensions and angers felt when the Territory was struggling toward statehood. There were divided opinions. The eastern half of the Territory, Cherokees and Choctaws principally, wanted their own state and wanted to call it Sequoyah. They wanted a line right down the middle of the Territory and the western half, as far as they were concerned, could have their own state and call it what they liked. My parents' sympathies were, inevitably, with the eastern Indians. "They were the first ones in the Territory," Lucy used to say, "and they were the most highly civilized. They paved the way for all the others. They printed the first books and newspapers and established the first schools. And they always had a high conception, once they had their land boundaries settled, of law and government. Politics stripped them of their rights and their authority. They were simply outpoliticked." She would shake her head.

The language of my childhood was full of soft French and Indian names. French trappers explored the country first and gave many streams and mountains their names. Among the rivers there were the Verdigris, the Illinois, the Fourche, the Cache, the Vache Gras, the Saliseau, and the mountain range that lay to our backs was called by them the Ouachita. We anglicized it to Washita.

The mountains that range across northwest Arkansas are the Ozarks, an anglicized version of Aux Arcs; and there was the tree which I learned to call the "bow-dark" and which some called hedge orange. Not until I was grown did I know it was the Bois d'arc. The Indians used it to make their bows.

Most of the towns had Indian names — Tishomingo, Tuskahoma, Pushmataha, Bokoshe, Muskogee, Hitchita, Weleetka, Okmulgee, Wewoka, Shawnee, Tahlequah, Checotah, Wapanucka, Pawhuska, Coweta, Seminole and Tecumseh, to name a few.

On one side of our town the prairie stretched endlessly, broken here and there by dry washes we called gullies and by a few trees and slight knolls. Behind us began the foothills of the Ouachita Mountains with their individual ranges, the Winding Stair, the Kiamichi, the Jack Fork and Pine Mountain and the lofty heads of Cavanal and Sugar Loaf.

That lovely long prairie was our backyard when I was a child. We were allowed to play on it as long as we didn't go beyond the first gully. That was still within sight of the house. But there was a skimpy grove of persimmons and blackjacks, enough to make shade, and under them we built playhouses and into them we climbed and occupied ourselves for hours at a time.

It would have been heaven except for one thing — my mother's whistle. She didn't bother to call us. She used my father's bird-dog whistle which had a blast so shrill and keen it carried for miles. After a few of my experiments with saying "I didn't hear you," she took to this whistle and it became the bane of my existence. Nobody could help hearing the dratted thing. One long blast meant me, me only, who had to leave all the others, perhaps a dozen, and trudge home, usually to "mind the baby." Two meant my sister and me and when the baby had become a toddler and we were compelled to take him with us, three meant all of us. And there was no arguing or dallying with a whistle. If it had to blow again, it meant a switching. That whistle said, "Come right this minute and on the double." I loathed it. And when I was seven, I think, it occurred to me one day to hide it.

I wasn't logical enough to drop it some place where, when it was found and even I knew it would inevitably be found — I was just bucking for as many days of peace and freedom as I could get — it might accidentally have fallen. I had to wedge it hard behind the doorjamb.

There were three heavenly days before she found it. The only weakness in my plot was my sister, Mary. Mary was a truly good child with a loving heart and an amiable disposition. I had to threaten her with all sorts of dire results if she told. Just the opposite of my sister, strong willed and stubborn, defiant and rebellious to the point of folly, I felt no shame at all over hiding the whistle. I was only afraid Mary would weaken.

It didn't come about that way. Lucy just got so provoked at its loss that one day she instigated a thorough search and of course she found it and of course she asked who hid it and of course (we never lied, not out of honor but because you got licked hardest of all for lying) I confessed. That might have been the end of it. Lucy might have scolded and warned and let it go. But from the day I was born there was a clashing of wills between Lucy McGraw and me because we are as much alike in temperament as two peas in a pod. We had the same flaring tempers, the same stubbornness, the same strong wills, the same toughness and resiliency and determination. I owe her much for these qualities because I survived many things in my adult life which might have defeated me had I not possessed them. I even had her same way of sticking my chin out. And I stuck it out too far that day. I stuck it out because when she found the whistle there was a sweet and secret exultation inside me. I had been the victor for three days. I had foiled her and bested her for three whole days and I was perfectly willing to take my punishment. It came immediately and I had trouble sitting the rest of the day.

But if my mother was like God (only more terrible because of her daily imminence) in her omnipotence she was like him also in her sheltering love. Ordinarily we might hide, wiggle away, evade, flee from, escape her, but came an injury, to flesh or spirit, and we could not rush swiftly enough to her. She was *there*, always, and she always knew what to do, and she always comforted and healed.

We were racing once, several neighbor children and ourselves, down the hard-baked road and in some manner Mary crossed in front of me and we became entangled. I recovered but she fell and she was running so hard that the impetus made her slide a long way with her arms outstretched before her. When we picked her up she was scratched and torn but what was worse a great gout of blood was gushing from her cut wrist. We screamed for Mama and took Mary home.

Lucy met us at the back door, took one look at Mary, said to my father, "Get the doctor," then calmly sat down on the porch steps, applied pressure to the severed artery to stop the bleeding, smoothed the hair back from the hot, tearstained small face pillowed in her lap, and talked quietly to us all — about what I do not now remember but it was so commonplace, so normal and ordinary and her voice was so quiet that our hearts were calmed and our fears were stilled and Mary stopped crying. It seemed a long, long time before my father came with the doctor and all that time my mother sat with her fingers stopping the arterial blood which, escaping, would have bled my sister to death.

She had no hand to calm the rest of us. She did it with her voice. When the doctor came he glanced at her. His eyes noted her pallor. "Go in the house, Lucy. John and I will take care of this."

He didn't suggest it but once. Her eyes flashed fire at him and she held her child while the artery was tied and the long gash stitched up. My father, who could never bear to see pain, had to turn away. Not Lucy. She sat with the screams in her ears and held the small arm tightly so the doctor could do his work and not until it was over and Mary was comforted with a licorice stick did she go silently behind the house and lose her supper.

And we always wanted to be with our parents at night. I never spent a night away from home as a child that I was not violently homesick, so homesick that often I vowed never to do it again. All children have that lost, uneasy feeling at night when away from home but we had more reason than most to feel it for the evenings in our family were very special.

Because my parents were teachers there was a sweet routine about it. When supper was over and the dishes done the big lamp was lit and set in the middle of the dining table. Five people sat around it studying, each in his own place never to be varied, my father and mother on one side, my sister and brother and I on the other. Besides the lamp there would be on the table bowls of apples and nuts, popcorn and, sometimes, homemade candy. We munched and studied. We couldn't persuade them to help us much. "Daddy, when was the Battle of Hastings?"

"There's the encyclopedia, Janice."

"But Daddy, *you* know. Tell me."

"Look it up for yourself."

Or Mary would say to Lucy, sighing, "Fractions are so hard!"

"Not if you've learned your rules. What are you doing?"

"Multiplication."

"Did you remember to invert?"

"Yes, ma'am."

"Then you didn't multiply correctly. Try again."

Or John, whimpering. "I *can't* do diagrams."

"Nonsense. Of course you can."

"But I can't remember the difference between prepositions and conjunctions."

"Then you didn't learn it. Find your definitions and study them."

Once in a while, once in a great, great while, we could

catch them so absorbed in the hundreds of papers they had to grade every night that absent-mindedly they would answer. But it didn't happen often. And we never dared dally or play around. There was a time limit on homework. If you weren't finished by nine o'clock it was just too bad. They knew it could be done by then and promptly at nine books were put away.

Then soft fleecy nightgowns were brought from the cold bedrooms and warmed by the fire. We were helped into them. Ready for bed we crowded onto laps and were held to warm our feet. Pillows were also warming behind the stove. Then, my father carrying two, my mother one, we were quickly tucked into bed. The door was left ajar, a sliver of light making a golden bar across our beds.

Then came the most perfect hour of the day. My father played the violin, my mother the piano. Settled in bed, snug, warm, safe beyond all measure of safety since, we listened nightly to their music. They played softly and quietly, but as long as one child was awake they played. Sometimes, thinking we were all asleep, they stopped only to have one plaintive voice call, "I'm not asleep yet." There was no quarrel with it, no impatience. There was only laughter and more music.

What a priceless treasure they gave us and we took it so for granted. We never knew if they were tired or ill or worried and they must have been all three often. No matter . . . it was the children's hour of music. However the heart ached or the head or the back, it was never allowed to interfere. But it must have had its own therapy for them too.

I remember our excitement the day the piano, a tremendously heavy ·oak upright, was delivered. I think I must have been six and none of us knew how we had come by it. Lucy earned it. She sold subscriptions to the Fort Smith newspaper. She must have sold subscriptions to everybody in a dozen counties and it must have taken her a year, but she did it. She was determined her children would have music in the home. My father *wished* we could have, but Lucy never stopped at wishing.

They had several ways of making the budget stretch during the lean months of the summer but their favorite was to head for the mountains and camp out all summer. Usually the John Snodgrasses went with us and with pooled resources an entire summer could be lived with very little money.

Before I was born the equipment for comfortable camping had been acquired — a big tent, bedrolls, a "grub box" which my father had fitted out so handily it made a kitchen cabinet when opened out. There was a dutch oven for baking, a spider for frying, a black kettle for boiling and stewing, and of course a big enamel coffeepot which was never empty.

The first camping trips were made with a wagon and team and Aunt Annabelle says she was foolish enough to take Robert when he was only ten months old. This was a hunting as well as fishing trip, way back in the mountains on the Jack Fork River. There were bear, deer, wild turkey and on the trail of something big the men wouldn't give up, so occasionally the men were away overnight.

One night when they were gone a violent thunderstorm blew up. Only those who have camped in the mountains can know how terrifying a storm can be there. The lightning seems brighter and more dangerous and the thunder seems more deafening and the wind, lashing the trees, seems to blow a gale.

Admittedly never brave physically, Aunt Annabelle gradually lost her courage. As the tent cracked and whipped in the wind, the lightning flared and the thunder rumbled and echoed from the canyons and peaks, she began to weep and pray. She and my mother, both past eighty now, tell it with loving laughter. "There I was," Aunt Annabelle says, "crying and moaning, vowing one minute never to let John Snodgrass hear the last of this trip with a baby, and the next minute praying, 'Lord, save my baby. Save my baby, Lord, *please* save my baby!' "

"What was Mother doing?"

"The sensible things. She was piling the bedrolls in dry places, putting buckets under the leaks, bracing the tent poles. Finally one corner of the tent collapsed and she had to go outside and peg it down again. She came in looking like a drowned rat and found me still wringing my hands and praying. She squeezed the water out of her hair and looked at me and then she said, 'Annabelle, if you've got to pray, get hold of that center pole and hold on to it and pray like hell for it not to give way. Your baby will be safe then.' "

"What did you do?"

"I grabbed hold of that center pole and held on to it and I prayed like hell for it not to give way!"

When we chuckle she looks at my mother, whom she loves devotedly. "I had to. Lucy would have killed me if I hadn't."

When we came along it never occurred to my father and mother to let us interfere with their camping fun. They just counted more noses and kept right on going. "You aren't going to take those children back into the mountains for the summer, are you?"

"Certainly. Why not?" I have heard Lucy reply.

"But what if there's an accident? What if they get sick?"

"Oh, well," my mother would say, "if you want to be all that cautious, they could always fall down the back steps and break their necks."

There was always a complete medical kit, of course. But my mother was largely the family doctor anyhow. Measles or pneumonia she would have handled competently and never lost a fish. Drowned, she would have resuscitated us, shot, she would have bandaged us. She had complete confidence in her own judgment and we had more faith in her than we had in the Lord. Lucy was *right there!*

But, when it came to building a house on top of water, however, I'm afraid not even Lucy's will would have been enough. Certainly mine was not. It took a big assist from Mister G.

Chapter 5
The Sink Goes Here

OUR DIFFICULTIES were happily in the future when we began, however. I thought our biggest problem would be the trees. There was obviously only one place to build the house — exactly where the little white farmhouse stood in the grove of huge sycamores and maples. It was a tight fit for the little farmhouse, though, and I began to cudgel my brains for a house plan that would be big enough for us and still miss the trees. It took some doing because this is a very nice grove of trees we have. There are grand huge sycamores, three graceful maples, several locusts, a box elder and a horn-beam, and a whole orchard full of apple trees. I didn't want to cut a tree, not only because they are beautiful and it's a sin to cut a tree, but because shade is the best possible insula-tion against Kentucky's summer sun.

The plan I finally came up with, and to which Mister G. dubiously agreed, was T-shaped with all ends and angles sheltered under the spreading trees. I would have liked to make the angles less square and let the house ramble a bit more freely and pleasantly but Mister G. reminded me we were building of logs and there were natural limitations to angling and rambling. Logs must be joined true.

The rough plan approved I set to work with as many of Mr. G.'s instruments as I knew how to use to make a blueprint — well, my kind of blueprint. It began with a huge piece of cardboard because I meant to draw the plans to a quarter-inch scale. I never could add and subtract fractions and even quarter inches would give me plenty of trouble but it would be the kiss of death for me to get involved in thirds and sixteenths and eighths. I really wanted to use an inch scale but Mister G. said they didn't make cardboard that big.

Only the Lord knows how many pieces of cardboard I ruined. Mister G. was still with the newspaper, the *Adair County News* in Columbia, now, and almost every night when he looked over what I had done during the day he found a glaring error. "You can't have a window there."

"Why not?"

"It's only a foot from the door."

"What's wrong with that?"

"Good Lord! *You're* the one who wants logs! Don't you know you can't just whittle logs into twelve-inch pieces and stick 'em in any old place? You've got to have *length* for strength. You want the walls to stay up, don't you? You'll have to put your window *here*."

"I can't. That's where the refrigerator goes."

"Then move the refrigerator."

"I can't. That's the only place it'll go."

"You mean to tell me that in a kitchen eighteen by twenty feet there is only *one* place the refrigerator will go? It's not possible."

But it *was* possible and any woman would have understood immediately. A housewife plans her kitchen around her own work habits and at my age I had had plenty of time to form some that were so routine I knew it would be traumatic to try to change them. The refrigerator goes *here*, the cooking counter goes *there*, the sink goes *here*, the dish cupboards go *there*, the stove goes *here*. I can cook a meal without moving more than two steps in any direction, if the arrangements are my own. And I got them. I just did without that window. The refrigerator definitely had to go *there*, and I could always turn on the light on dark days.

But Mister G. was wrong about having to have length for strength. When the house was finished we wound up with *two* doors, count them, *less* than twelve inches from corners and it was none of my doing. And the walls haven't come tumbling down yet.

After using almost all the cardboard in the *Adair County News*'s stockroom I eventually came up with a plan which placed all doors and windows, indicated all closets and cabinets and cupboards, electrical outlets and even the bathroom fixtures. It was the only blueprint the men ever had. I don't know what ever happened to it. Wanting to preserve it for posterity after the house was completed I looked and looked for it and it has never, to this good day, come to light. I think Mister G. burned it along toward the last out of sheer frustration. I had hauled it around incessantly proving things. "See. Here on the plan, it's plain. The door goes *here*. Why are you putting it there?"

After the first few times he didn't trouble to explain why

about anything. He just grunted at me, which I took to mean shut up and get out of the way.

The Plan was helpful, however, in determining how many sets of logs we needed. We had one set already, the fishing camp. And if anybody wants to know why, since we had a log fishing camp, we didn't simplify the whole process by building our house around it instead of taking it down and moving it, let me simply say the fishing camp was in *Green County!* Fine for a fishing camp but no place for an Adair Countian to live.

It was a handsome, spacious cabin built from an excellent set of poplar logs. It was eighteen by twenty-two feet and a story and a half in height. Originally it had been a Negro church in the community of Hibernia, in Taylor County. It had long been abandoned when it was bought, taken down and moved to the banks of Green River. Now we proposed to take it down and move it again. If we were going to live within sight of the river in Adair County we knew we'd never use the camp again. And we doubted we could sell it. We had tried to sell it before and found no takers. So we meant to make it our living room in the new home. Few people have a living room that cost $2600 before it ever got off the ground, but we do. It's a doubtful distinction.

The Plan called for five rooms, entrance hall and bath downstairs and three dormer bedrooms upstairs. Mister G. can go into bitter details about why we ended up with five rooms, entrance hall and bath downstairs all right, but with nothing but attic space overhead. It has something to do with a sudden soaring of my spirits which took wild wings one day and asked that all the ceilings be raised one foot!

It had been agreed that the living room, the master bedroom, and the kitchen, would be built of logs. The middle section, joining the two ends of the house, would not be. Mister G. was so grateful that any part of the house would be more flexible than logs that he barely winced when I suggested a rough-sawed board and batten exterior. "It shouldn't be painted at all," I said. "It should be allowed to weather. In time it will be the same soft gray as the logs."

"I suppose you know," he growled, "you're making us the laughingstock of the country."

I did know it. Few people care for a log house any more and even fewer think them beautiful. The ranch house has invaded the Kentucky hills with just as much deadliness and monotony as it did the plains and prairies it was more suited to. I knew it would be only a handful of people who would understand at all what we were doing. To most, we appeared foolish and queer. Remarks had been reported to me. "With the same money they could build a real nice house."

"It'll look just like a barn."

"Wouldn't give you a dime for a log house."

I didn't want anybody to give a dime for it. I didn't ask anybody to live in it and didn't care whether they did or not. And I couldn't have cared less what they thought. It was our house and it was our business how we built it. But my goodness gracious, if Frank Lloyd Wright had hung one of his cliff dwellings from the hills it wouldn't have caused more curiosity and comment. "Do you mind if they laugh?" I asked Mister G.

He grinned. "Nope. I'm betting on you and I'll bet they come from miles to see your log house when it's finished."

And that's just what they do.

"We have the living room," Mister G. said one day, "so we'll only need three more sets of logs."

"Two," I corrected, "one for the bedroom and one for the kitchen."

"Three," he insisted firmly, "one for the bedroom, one for the kitchen, and one for patching."

Patching? I hadn't known you could patch. I found it very interesting. If we could patch, maybe I could move a few doors and windows around. He vetoed that notion promptly. Patching, he explained, was only replacement. In a set of logs invariably there would be several in which decay would be too far gone. They must be replaced with good logs. My vision of more doors and windows faded.

"Where," a friend asked, "are you going to find all those logs?"

"We'll be buried under them," I told her, "once the word gets out."

I knew how the grapevine worked. We had only to tell half a dozen people we were looking for logs (and you might narrow that down safely to three, or two, or even one, if you told the right person) and everybody who had two poplar logs ready to be chopped into kindling wood would get in touch with us. There aren't as many log sets as there used to be but there are still hundreds of abandoned log cabins in our three adjoining counties. They are usually used as barns until they fall in beyond usefulness when they are split up and burned on tobacco beds.

It came about as I had said. Our mail suddenly began to be flooded with offers from as far away as Hart County, and people flocked to tell us of a cabin they owned in Taylor County, or Green County, in Casey County, in Russell County, and all about us in Adair County.

We didn't want to move log houses any farther than we

had to, so we ruled out everything outside our own county.

It was the tail end of summer and both the thermometer and the humidity stood at a sweltering ninety-five when Mister G. took a vacation from newspapering to command the search for the logs and to oversee the moving of them. He had incorporated a cousin, Edgar Giles, into the project and the three of us flowed liquidly, swimming in a stream of our own sweat, over all the acres of our county. I don't know what plagued us most, the heat, sweat in our eyes, blackberry brambles, stick-tights and beggarlice, or the constant threat of snakes. Some of the old log sets were grown to the eaves in brambles and weeds, their stone chimneys only a pile of rubble, and this is copperhead and rattlesnake country. Edgar and Mister G. always carried heavy, knobby sticks that could kill with the first blow, and we all wore jeans and boots. The men always plowed through the debris first to flush out any lurking reptiles, but I never got over a strong desire to find a high stump and stand there with my jeans hoisted. Mice and snakes are both deadly enemies as far as I'm concerned, though either may be and usually are perfectly harmless.

In a country house there is eternal war with mice in the cupboards and it is always me that puts an unsuspecting hand into a drawer and touches that cold, furry little field mouse that has crept in. Having lived with me for four years in the city where never a mouse showed his little beady black eyes, Mister G. was wholly unprepared for my reaction the first time this happened. He heard a high, wild screech, followed by lunatic yelps for help, and he came pounding into the kitchen, his heart thudding, expecting to find I had cut a hand off or poured a skillet of hot grease down my bosom.

What he found was his wife standing on top of the kitchen counter jibbering like an idiot at a tiny brown field mouse that was so out of its own mind with fear it was running in circles around the floor.

He has never quite grown accustomed to the commotion that results when I find a mouse, but he *has* learned to look for me somewhere near the ceiling. I just climb the nearest thing.

I have the same reaction to snakes, even the most innocent and common garden varieties. If it slithers on its belly and darts a forked tongue at me, it's dangerous and I don't want any long acquaintance with it.

We had many more snakes on the ridge than we have here in the valley, but I think my worst experience with one occurred after we had moved into the new house. I was spring-housecleaning and Mister G. had gone up to the schoolhouse, which we use as a storehouse and catchall. I stepped outside the kitchen onto the back stoop to shake out a small rug. From the corner of my eye I caught a movement as the screen door shut behind me, then unbelievably I saw it was a small snake caught by the door, its head on the outside of the door, its tail frantically flailing the air on the inside.

Well, I had it caught firmly. All I had to do was wedge the door more tightly to choke it to death, but as usual I panicked. I did manage to look at it more closely and it looked exactly like a small copperhead to me, the brown diamonds, the flat head, the rough scaly look and all. Sometime before, our hound, Ring, had been bitten by a copperhead and Mister G. had been a little uneasy that the snake may have been somewhere near the house. The dog roams the hills and we both knew he had probably been bitten up there, but with his head already swelling and his body already stiffening, he had gone to find Mister G. and he had come from the direction of the house. Neither of us said so, but what we feared, what all country people fear, was that a copperhead had somehow got *under* the house. Now, staring at that vile little snake caught in the screen door I was certain of it and I was certain, furthermore, that it had been a female copperhead and she had nested and brought forth young and this little venomous thing, from its position with its head outside the door as if it had been crawling out, had been lurking somewhere *in* my kitchen! Nothing, literally nothing, could have made me go back inside the house.

Yelping like a scalded cat I jumped the creek in one bound and tore out across the pasture to the schoolhouse. When I got there, Mister G. was nowhere to be found. I took the lane this time but ran every step, stopped at one neighbor's house and found them away, and went on to Mister Ancil Spires's house. Mister Ancil is fragile and old, but at least he was a man and some man certainly had to come and kill that snake.

Both he and Miss Martha came home with me. And I would like to say right here that Mister Ancil approached his killing job with a considerable amount of caution. He found the hoe, crept up on the snake, firmly applied pressure on the screen door until the snake stopped wiggling, then he lifted it out into the yard with the hoe. He thought it was a copperhead, too.

He and Miss Martha both went into the house with me and we took it apart drawer by drawer, cupboard by cupboard, closet by closet, bed by bed. We found nothing. But we were all disturbed by the position of the snake. We could make nothing of it except that it had been caught crawling out of the house. But there were obviously no more inside. With our own eyes we had proved that. There was no point in Mister Ancil and Miss Martha staying longer so they went home.

When Mister G. returned an hour later he found me sitting like Buddha on the kitchen table trying to ease my shakes with a good-sized slug of bourbon on the rocks!

The next hour, when Mister G. slithered around on his own belly under the house (a thorough and complete search had to be made, of course) was one of the worst times I ever expect to live through, even with a bourbon anesthetic. When he came out finally, shaking his head, the relief was so great I did what all women do when the crisis is over. I dissolved into tears.

Had the snake been full grown Mister G. and the neighbors could have told immediately whether or not it was a copperhead. But neither he nor they had seen many baby copperheads so the opinions were varied. Some said it was a copperhead, others said no, it was a viper. This is a harmless adder we have around here which does resemble a copperhead to a surprising degree. We never had a majority opinion either way and to this good day don't really know what it was. Neither did we ever solve the problem of the snake's position. It was studied, measured and debated, to no conclusion. It *may* have been in the house. On the other hand the screen may have caught it and swiveled it around. It remains a mystery, and I do despise things I can't pin down!

So as we approached all these weedgrown sets of logs that summer I felt gingerly apprehensive and I exercised much caution. But they had to be looked at and examined and tested and sounded for termites and rot.

The most perfect set we found, the most beautiful, was not far away. It was the old home of Mr. Jonce Ferguson, hidden away at the mouth of a hollow with a great cliffy hill at its back. It had three log rooms, instead of the usual one, and except for the kitchen it was still in excellent condition. The kitchen, separate from the other rooms by a dogtrot, had fallen in.

Mister Jonce had not built it. It was much older than he and it was the home of the family from whom he bought it. But it became his home and his children grew up in it.

Whoever built it was not simply an exquisite craftsman, he was an artist. No other set we looked at had such beautiful locking notches, so true, so carefully hewn and set logs. And we never saw again such precise, axed, four-by-four rafters, pegged in with carefully whittled wooden pegs. Even the sheathing was pegged on. Nor were we ever again to see logs so smooth and satiny. Outside they were like gray satin. Inside they were glowingly mellow, with dark gold overtones. It was enough to make you catch your breath. It was pure sculpture and one thought instantly of Michelangelo and the *pietra serena*, the serene stone, of the Tuscan hills. These great, solid poplar logs had been chiseled by a hand that loved wood, that handled it fondly, held it in respect and formed it into beauty.

But it was not to be ours and nothing else in our building hurt me quite so much as to have to turn my back on it. I wanted so badly to have our house honored by the work of that old craftsman that it was a physical pain in my chest for days.

Mister Jonce was using the old house for a barn. He saw no way to let us have it unless we could provide him with a barn to take its place. I would have been willing but Mister G. said it would be folly. A barn as large as the house, built to his specifications, would have cost too much. No set of logs, Mister G. said, was worth that. We could find all too many sets for as little as twenty-five dollars. "We've got a $2600 living room," he said, "and we can't possibly afford a $1500 kitchen."

I could have. To me values are relative. A few years ago my son-in-law was able finally to acquire a certain lot in Santa Fe after years of looking at it longingly each time he drove past it. He paid an enormous amount for it and many people thought him foolish to do it. I did not, for I believed his yearning for it, his deep desire for it, made it worth any amount to him. To me, Mr. Jonce Ferguson's logs would have come cheap at the cost of a new barn and I still regret that I didn't go stubborn and bullheaded and insist on buying them.

Mister Jonce could spare the kitchen logs, since they had fallen in, and we took them. But they were much smaller than any others we eventually found and we could only use them for patching. I think we have two of them some place in the house.

As with the logs of the Jonce Ferguson house, the chimney was also a work of art. Each rock had been carefully chosen, then perfectly chiseled and squared, placed flat and true on the other. We asked about buying the chimney. We had a stone chimney at the fishing camp, but it was limestone. These rocks were the soft yellow fieldstone that can look so like marble.

Mister Jonce didn't think he had better let us have the chimney, either. Taking it out would weaken the house and leave an immense hole he'd have to shore up. I began to wish we had never seen the Jonce Ferguson place since it seemed we could have none of it. I thought it would have been better for my peace of mind never to have known it existed than to go looking for logs and chimneys which, by comparison to it, seemed so crude and unformed.

It was by accident, or an irony of fate, that the stone chimney did finally come to us. About the time we began the actual building of the house there was a violent wind- and rain-storm, one of the worst in years. The old chimney which had withstood thousands of wind- and rain-storms in its time and which looked so eternal and immovable did not withstand this latest storm. It swayed away from its companion logs, cracked, and fell into rubble. Word was sent to us, now, that we could have it if we still wanted it. We might not have taken it down so abruptly and unlovingly but we would certainly have had to take it down to move it, so the fact that it had fallen did not disturb us and we did still want it. I could not help feeling the Lord meant me to have that chimney and while he took a rather violent way of giving it to me I had no complaints.

Across the river and not far away we found another good set of logs, though it was a single set instead of a double as the Jonce Ferguson place had been. We drove down a lane, then forsook the car and plodded across a field to the edge of the woods. The lean-to room, which in the old days was always added after several years of living in one room, had fallen in but the log set was in good condition and the logs were yellow poplar, the kind we had to have. This structure

was being used as a sort of overflow storage place for hay.
It wasn't really needed by the owner. A price was quoted —
thirty-five dollars, and we said we'd take the set and we'd
have a man there the following week to begin taking it down.

I hope I won't be accused of injustice to my fellowman
when I say that over and over again we have had the interesting but disillusioning experience of having a price hiked
on us when people learned who was buying. People think
we are either rich or foolish, or both. We are neither, I
hope, to the extent of being gulls.

Later, I badly wanted old hand-blown glass windowpanes
for the house. There arc many to be found in abandoned
old homes or stacked away and forgotten in old barns and
storehouses. We found enough in one deserted old house to
furnish every window in ours. In their exquisite flawed
beauty they were simply lying there, being broken by vandals,
sagging to the ground and breaking as they fell. A few more
years and nothing would be left of them. A friend of ours
spoke to the owner for us.

The man cogitated for a while then grinned and said,
"Think I'll not set a price right now. Let 'em hurt a while.
Them folks'll pay ten times what they're worth when they've
hurt enough."

This was pure chicanery. This was the kind of greedy
meanness that raises the hackles on my neck and which I
refuse to gratify. We not only did not hurt over the bub-
bled panes, we wouldn't have had them as a precious gift
from a man with that attitude. I couldn't have enjoyed them.
Every time I looked through them some of his poison would
spill over onto me.

We were to suspect something of the same sort now with

the cabin across the river. Word was sent to us that "Ma," who had quoted the price, didn't understand that a new tin roof had been put on the cabin just a few years before and that a new floor had been laid not long before that, and that the family just didn't see how they could sell the logs without getting some of their money back on the roof and floor. The family didn't see how they could sell for the price "Ma" had quoted.

We had a strong feeling that the family had decided the G.s would pay a lot more than thirty-five dollars, but we asked what they felt a fair price would be. After some indecision it was given as one hundred dollars.

Because there was to some extent reason here which went beyond suspicion, though there was enough of that, we agreed to pay the hundred dollars. The cabin *did* have a good roof on it and the flooring *was* good, and while we wanted neither it was certainly true their usefulness to the owner would be finished when we took the logs away. But I must admit those logs don't look as beautiful to me as some of the others in the house and it is not my imagination, Mister G. will also vouch for it, they creak and complain considerably more than any of the others!

We found our third set of logs standing tall and lonely in a field on a farm near Columbia. It, too, had been used as a barn but the new owner now meant to tear it down. We were just in time. He was going to burn a plant bed with them.

Next to the Jonce Ferguson logs these were the biggest, the best, and the prettiest, we had found. I think the owner might have given them to us, but he took twenty-five dollars for them and was delighted to have them hauled away.

I wished, many times, looking at these old log houses that I hadn't been so imaginative. The life they had once pulsed with pressed in hard on me and I was continually being hurt by their abandonment. I never looked at one without thinking about the births and deaths, the laughter and tears, the griefs and joys the old log walls had witnessed. Touching a pale, ancient log, feeling it solid beneath my hand, I sensed its contact with life, its mute testimony. It had survived, in most instances, the human hands that had hewed it. The four walls had closed round a family, cherished and protected it, and now they housed nothing but snakes and rats and loose hay and grain. Children had been conceived and born in this home. The logs had heard hungry squalls and witnessed their hushing at the mother's breast. They had been lit by candle glow and oil lamps and they had reflected the faces of the well and happy, the ill and dying. They had looked upon a family at meals, at work, quarreling perhaps occasionally, laughing together when temper was over, loving and living.

But a log house is not everybody's cup of tea and to be able to build new, say goodbye to the old, is nearly always a prestige and status symbol, to say nothing, in the case of growing families, of being a necessity.

I learned a strange thing when our house was finished and we had moved into it. Logs a hundred and fifty years old are still alive. They aren't dead. They are a little restless and they move slightly and they speak. There are queer sounds from them in the night, whispers and creaks and little jolts and thuds. To me they are friendly sounds as if the logs were putting their heads together and talking over old times, exchanging reminiscences, brooding over us perhaps, like an old mother hen, smoothing their feathers for the night.

Sometimes I do a foolish thing and give an old log one last pat as I go to bed. As with children I try to have no favorites. They are all good, sturdy logs. But there are several that are so beautiful I can't help beaming upon them, and I am compelled to touch them more often than the others. And I can't help feeling they are the ones that really hold the house together.

Chapter 6
We Didn't Reverse Enough

WE SPENT the summer in the small farmhouse the Spireses had built, partly to be near our base of operations but chiefly so the grandsons could pay their usual visit.

The youngest, who is nothing if not frank, looked around with wide eyes at the sloped floors, the canted walls, the sagged ceilings, whistled and said, "Gosh, don't anybody blow a trumpet! These walls'll come tumbling down."

The house was to be torn down at the end of the summer to make way for the new house but even so Mister G. thought a new "necessary" was needed. The boys arrived a little early, however, and before it was completed. Nature therefore required us to use the old structure for a few days. The first time Scott had to go he came back with his nose wrinkled. "May I have a clothespin, please?"

Knowing very well what for, but wanting to hear what he'd say, I asked, "What for?"

"To hang on a nail out there so's people won't have to smell."

Scott is the young man who decided very early in his life to be an archeologist. "If," he adds realistically, "there's anything left to archeologize by the time I'm grown."

"Why do you want to be an archeologist?" we ask.

"Two reasons," he replies brightly. "I like to extravate and I like to sleep late."

We could understand his enjoyment of excavating but he didn't get through to us with that bit about sleeping late. "What does sleeping late have to do with archeologizing?"

"Well, golly," he explains, "if the stuff's been buried a million years already there's no use getting up at seven o'clock in the morning to dig!"

All three grandsons throw long words around like a cat by the tail and always have. Sometimes, in fact usually, they have no idea what a word means and their pronunciation is nearly always off, but they love the sound of them just the same. Bart, the oldest, was precisely three years old when my daughter said to my mother, "Lucy, we'll have to marry Bart off *very* young so you can have great-great-grandchildren too."

We were at the dinner table. Bart lifted his nose out of his plate and said with icy dignity, "You will not! I do not plan to be an ancestor!"

He is also the one who said, at two and a half, on a sigh when reproved, "Life is *so* difficult!"

At considerable expense and inconvenience to themselves my daughter and her husband have shared the boys with us generously each summer since they were big enough to haul around. When they were still babies Libby used to come with them.

I have one fabulous memory of the first visit.

We met them at the airport. Bart must have been three, Mike would have been two, and Scott was a bare ten months. The big plane circled and landed, then taxied up to the gate. Almost beside myself with eagerness I watched as the passengers disembarked. They came and they came and they came, but no Libby and babies. Finally, and a long time after everyone else was off the plane, the pilot stepped out carrying Bart. The co-pilot followed bearing Mike. The stewardess emerged with Scott and a distraught and disheveled Libby brought up the rear burdened with bundles and bags and bottles.

It had been a nightmare of a journey of course. Both Bart and Mike were ambulatory and Libby told a hilarious tale of precisely how ambulatory they had been the entire eight hours. This was before the days of jets and she had unfortunately caught a slow freight. It seemed that the crew and all the passengers had had to come to her assistance, not only in the interest of peace, but in the interest of safety as well. At a strategic moment Bart was discovered trying to work the emergency door and it was soul-shaking to think what might have happened had he been a little taller and a little stronger.

All three babies had been airsick, not once but several times, and often two at the same time. "After several disasters," Libby said, her sense of humor still intact, "everybody on the plane took to watching for green-faced babies. Before I'd notice somebody would yell, 'The middle boy, lady, the middle boy!' And the stewardess would lope up the aisle with another nosebag. We used up the normal supply in the first hundred miles and the greatest anxiety of everybody on board was that we'd use up the entire stock before it could be replenished."

With two babies erping at the same time, the third was bound to get away. Mike came up missing after one such incident. A general search was organized. Seats were peered under, the lavatory explored, even the luggage rack was probed. By now everybody knew that nothing was impossible for the two babies that could walk. The missing child could be in the most unlikely place and wherever he was he was bound to be doing something that might be fatal either to himself or the plane.

Here let me say that I wrote a short story once about the doings of the three boys when they had got a little older. A magazine editor who saw it was affronted by what she called my wild imagination. "No children," she stated categorically, "behave like that."

Ours did. I hadn't imagined one single little incident of that story. In their time they have tried to clean the toilet with the vacuum cleaner, with such preposterously chaotic results that nobody could have imagined it. It had to be seen to be believed. Scott, who was a baby then, was ill and the pediatrician was there. Libby had been using the vacuum cleaner and unfortunately she left it plugged in. Naturally she accompanied the doctor to Scott's bedside. When the explosion occurred the doctor sprang into the hall — suspecting an atom bomb, very likely — took one wild unbelieving look and exclaimed, "God! That's the worst case of diarrhea I ever saw!" It took days to clean the walls!

They once built a bonfire in the garage. If you wonder where they got the materials for a bonfire, they emptied the kitchen trash can and supplemented its contents with a few slats from a dismembered orange crate. When the fire was blazing they climbed on staggered tables and took down from the wall a mounted antelope head which was their father's pride and joy. This they proceeded to roast in the flames. No great damage was done except to the antelope head. It was reduced to two beady glass eyes and a singed mustache, but for weeks the entire estate smelled of scorched hair.

One time Bart melted the tines of a sterling silver fork in an electrical outlet. It shook him considerably and he is still of the opinion electricity isn't to be trusted.

Mike crawled in the washer-dryer on another memorable day and Bart slammed the door on him and pushed a button. Fortunately it was the "agitate" button, so he was neither laundered nor drowned. He was only spun dry.

Their father likes to hunt and he has quite a valuable and extensive arsenal which he very carefully keeps under padlock. How and where Bart and Mike found a handful of bullets to drop down the furnace grating nobody has ever been able to discover, but they did. The boys were slightly astonished but deeply gratified by what happened shortly thereafter but their mother was jolted into climbing the walls. She thought the Russians had attacked.

One of the more shocking experiences came when Scott became a kleptomaniac for one short week. He must have been about four and, since he was lonely at home with his older brothers in school, we took him with us wherever we went.

After a trip to the grocery store one day we found half a dozen unpaid-for candy bars in his pocket. His mother reproved him mildly and called the store to have the amount added to her account.

On the very next trip to the grocery two bags of jelly beans were discovered in his pocket, one badly plundered, the other intact. He was made, rather tearfully and bewilderedly, to return the unbroken bag and this time given the money to pay for the half-eaten bag.

The third time in almost as many days we had not yet driven away from the store when we noticed Scott, on the back seat, placidly munching away on animal crackers. His mother exploded. "Scott, when you take things you don't pay for it's stealing!"

His brown eyes, so like his mother's, rounded. "But, Mother, you don't pay for your things either."

Exasperated she said, "I certainly do. At the end of every month your daddy writes a check . . ."

She stopped and we stared at each other, sudden understanding breaking through. Charge accounts and checks were not part of Scott's experience. To him here was a whole, huge, wonderful store full of fine good things through which his mother wandered at will, helped herself, and apparently walked out of without paying. To pay, as far as he was concerned, was to hand over cash money. And what was sauce for the goose was sauce for the gander. He took what he wanted just as he had seen his mother take, and he came out loaded.

There was a fine lesson in the credit system which underlies the American economy right then and there you may be sure. Scott was fascinated and nothing pleased him more thereafter than to take his goods to the counter, display them proudly, and watch carefully until the checker had entered them in his mother's account book. In fact, it took all hands and the cook to keep him from buying out the entire store.

I would battle like a fighting cock at the suggestion they were bad boys, as this magazine editor intimated, when they were small, or even that they were undisciplined. In all the things that count they were good and honorable and gallant. They might conk a playmate over the head, or turn a hose on a neighbor dressed for a party, or, flowers were free weren't they? pick a bouquet for their lovely mother from a neighbor's prize tulip bed, but they wouldn't lie about what they had done and they took punishment well. They were simply supercharged. Put a tornado of energy inside a small boy, power it with a quick intelligence and a lively curiosity, to say nothing of superior inventiveness, and there's bound to be some destruction. Not everyone agreed with me, of course. There were those who honestly believed my daughter had three juvenile delinquents on her hands. I am happy to say that in their teens they have justified our faith and proved their detractors wrong. They are today three fine and gallant young gentlemen.

Mike was discovered eventually, the day he got lost on the plane, on the flight deck. It couldn't happen today, but from the co-pilot's lap he beamed at his mother and chortled happily, "I'm flying, see? I'm flying the plane!"

And he was allowed to "fly it" until he went to sleep.

"We can't possibly," my daughter moaned when she had finished her tale of woe, "use the return half of our tickets. That airline won't ever let us on their planes again."

But they did and for all I know it may have been the same crew. The kind of men who would let a little towheaded two-year-old with a wide grin and fetching blue eyes crawl into their laps and think he was flying the plane, keep him interested for an hour until he fell asleep, then carry him back to deposit carefully by his mother's side, aren't easily put out. And the kind of stewardess who leaped with a nosebag at each hiccup, who bathed foreheads and heated bottles and read stories aloud, may have been doing her duty but nothing required her to have sweet concern. "Poor babies, poor babies," she said, over and over.

It may have been quite a trip for them but I'd guess only a few grouchy passengers were really vexed.

My daughter made several such journeys home with them, then most of their flying difficulties were over. Her husband acquired a plane himself and from then on he delivered his sons to us personally. And their mother's presence was no longer required.

There began a series of halcyon summers for us, then, when we were permitted to have the boys for as long as two months at a time, and there began for their parents some free, unworried, unhampered vacation times.

They were six, five and three the first time we had them without a parent. We were living on the big farm and they ran wild over the meadows and fields and through the woods, in the barns and down the hillows. They had their baths daily in Green River which they thought was going swimming. They took turns riding the tractor with Mister G. whom they called Himmie. He was their stepgrandfather but they didn't know anything about that at the time.

It had eventually to be revealed to them when they were old enough to ask their mother, "When you were little did Himmie spank you?" "Did Himmie make you eat everything on *your* plate?" "Did you ride Himmie's horse on the farm when you were a little girl?"

A little fearfully she broke the news to them that Himmie

was not her own father. That didn't bother them. Her father could have been the czar of the Russias for all they cared, but it sure threw a monkey wrench in the works when it dawned on them Himmie was not their own grandfather! Next to their parents they adored him and I am not at all sure that at certain stages of their development he didn't come first.

They resolved this problem in their own way. They refused to have any part of this "step" business. Himmie was their own grandfather and no foolishness about it. "And," Mikey said gloweringly as if somebody meant to threaten him, "he is my favoritest grandfather in the *whole, wide world!*" From that position they never retreated and to the best of my knowledge the matter has never come up again.

That first summer there were chickens and calves, cows, pigs, and best of all a sorrel horse named Charlie. For city children, it was paradise. Of course there were the usual contretemps. All three got poison ivy in the worst possible place. Mister G. had taught them the virtues of a broad leaf when caught unprepared for nature while on a fishing expedition. Entranced they never again wanted to carry a roll of toilet paper in the car. But they mistook their leaves, with humiliating results.

Because they were so modest that they blushed at the very idea of a woman applying salve, Mister G. had to line them up in a private place each night, turn them one at a time over his knee and anoint their behinds. The most outrageous whoops and shouts used to come from behind the closed door and I strongly suspected some man-to-man and slightly off-color confidences going on.

They identified strongly with every living thing on the farm. Rosie's little black calf, which they inspected when it was only five minutes old (and would have ushered into the world if we hadn't arrived from town a few seconds too late) was the most beautiful calf in the world. They gave it a name, Blackie, I think, which was obvious, and they curried it and combed it and thought Mister G. very cruel to pull it away from the mother's udder after a few minutes of feeding.

They were torn between loyalty to the old Hampshire Red rooster, Chanticleer, and admiration for the beautiful young Black Minorca, Smoky Joe. In a moment of madness Mister G. had allowed the Minorca to grow up and become a rooster. Chanticleer had been the ruler of his harem too long to take this kindly. What it did to him suddenly to find himself with a rival cannot adequately be told. Eventually — and thank heaven the boys had gone home — it made a neurotic of him and drove him to suicide. Literally. He grew so incensed one day, went so berserk, that he burst a blood vessel and died of a massive cerebral hemorrhage.

The boys took a partisan interest in the pigs and were indignant that the runt should be always shoved aside. They thought the mother very neglectful not to take better care of him. "Can't she *see* he's the littlest?" We didn't tell them Mister G. had barely saved him from being eaten by her shortly after his birth. They wouldn't have survived the shock.

Of all the animals on the farm, however, they loved most the horse. We had bought him especially for them. With mechanical equipment, a horse we didn't need! But Mister G. felt strongly that all boys should have a horse. He was old, though not decrepit, and he was slightly lame. He was fat and he was so gentle they could clamber all over him, tumble about under him, hang on to his tail or mane, maul him or love him, and he just stood patiently and allowed it.

We had a bridle but no saddle. The horse was so gentle the boys could catch him by the mane and lead him to the barn. Bart soon mastered the difficulties of putting the bridle on him, then he would be led to a high stump in the back yard which made an excellent mounting block. Mister G. restricted their riding to the orchard and the yard, which gave them about three acres to roam about in. They rode happily for hours every day. Mostly Charlie walked, but occasionally they could kick him into a slow, lethargic trot. And all was well. Until they saw their first horse show at the county fair.

We had no idea the dissatisfaction it created in them. We used to see the three of them cluster together eying the horse but we weren't taken into their confidence. After the horse show they believed passionately and loyally that Charlie was so beautiful he must certainly have been a show horse at one time. Without understanding it at all they had picked up quite a horse vocabulary from having lingered around the stalls at the fair. "Just look at his withers," they would say about Charlie, "and his fetlocks."

"And just look at his compromise!" Scott chimed in.

It took us a little while to come up for air on that one. Not until I recalled that a horse's conformation was important in winning blue ribbons did we make it out.

We should have had some hint of how deeply they had been impressed when Mikey moaned at supper one night, "Charlie's tail is just beautiful but it isn't long enough!"

"My goodness," I burbled innocently, "didn't you know those were false tails on the show horses? No horse has a tail that long. They tie another tail onto the horse's real tail."

I don't know what Charlie thought about the addition to his tail the next day but I do know his gain was my loss.

They waited until after supper to exhibit Charlie in his new glory. This was their usual time for theatrical productions, which were an almost daily affair. It always cost us a nickel each to sit on our own front steps and watch a three-act play, or a circus, or a puppet show, or whatever. But the horse show was an innovation.

You can bet we were properly impressed, however, as Charlie, mounted by three small boys, slowly went through his paces — all two of them, walk and trot — with a long gray switch that looked for all the world as if it had been made of Brillo dangling from his tail.

Mister G. gave a convulsive heave, snorted once, cleared his throat and maintained calm. Behind his hand he whispered, though, "What *is* that stuff? Where did they get it?"

I didn't know yet but suspicion was dawning. Only that morning at breakfast I had said, aloud unfortunately, "Do you know, I believe that old sofa we bought at the auction sale the other day is stuffed with horsehair?"

After the horse show, which went off beautifully, I verified my suspicions. The old sofa was no longer stuffed with anything.

One of their most successful productions that summer was a play, full three acts naturally. It was called "The Rescue of the North Pole." Understand, we had no part in these productions except to be the audience. Theirs were the ideas, theirs the writing, theirs the producing, the staging, the acting. The whole idea was to put on a show which would be a complete surprise for us. Whatever weird or crazy thing they required in making their props, I tried to supply without questioning. No more than they did I want the element of surprise ruined.

Bart, the oldest, was always the master of ceremonies. Behind a huge japonica bush was the dressing room. Entries were always made from behind it, exits were made toward it. There was no such thing as Stage Left or Stage Right. There was only Stage Japonica Bush.

"The Rescue of the North Pole," Bart told us, was a melodrama in three acts. The first act took place on the Arctic Ocean. Exit master of ceremonies.

A frantic scurrying and placing of props followed. With no curtain, we were told to hide our eyes. Allowed to open them finally we viewed the bathtub, an elongated zinc oval, in center stage, with an oar dangling from the stern. A stepladder was amidships. An abandoned well bucket, of the tubular type, was laid across the bows. Scott, all three years of him, was perched atop the stepladder, a lard bucket overturned on his head, peering across the frozen wastes. Below, Bart and Mike — also with overturned lard bucket helmets — peered too. "Mate!" Bart bellowed, "what do you see?"

From the crow's nest Scott bellowed back, "Nothing but ice, sir."

"It *must* be there. The President says the North Pole has come loose. It's floating in the Arctic Ocean. Our mission is to find it."

Mike, who was lacking lines, belched.

"Yes, sir," came Scott's crisp reply.

All peered.

Suddenly Scott's voice rose in anguish. "Sir! A whale to starboard!"

Bart came to attention and his captainly decision was roared. "Man the guns!"

Mike saluted and uttered his first line. "Yes, sir."

He flew to the well pump, swiveled it and stuttered a staccato machine-gun fire at the whale. "Bbbbtttrrrr-bbbtttrrr-bbbtttrrr!"

He blasted that whale right out of the ocean and then reported to the captain, "The danger has been abberted, sir!"

"Very good."

End of Act I.

Act II was a pantomime. The three rescuers were obviously too weak to speak. They were in camp on the frozen wastes and had been reduced to boiling their boots for food. At one point I thought Scott was surely dying.

Act III began with the three weary explorers slogging it over the snow and ice dragging a sled behind them. They were almost exhausted. They tugged and hauled at the sled (the wheelbarrow minus its wheel) and beat their brows. Suddenly Mike, given a decent line at last, pulled up short, peered from under his palm and straightened his shoulders. "Sir! There it is! There's the North Pole!"

The captain had to exit suddenly to shove a pole embedded in a tub of sand onto the stage. The tub didn't slide very well, got hung up, and all three explorers had to abandon their roles to get it into position. But dignity was restored immediately. The flag of the United States rose in the air, three young explorers saluted, and the captain vociferated, "The President of the United States will give us medals for this, lads. The honor of the United States has been vinnicated!"

Later I was paying flattering compliments. Scott was modest. "It wasn't so hot," he said. "We didn't reverse enough."

It may have been that summer, or perhaps it was the next, we had the elegant funeral.

A hen who had hidden out her nest suddenly brought forth a hatch of six young chickens. One of them was a weakling. He wasn't long for this world. But Mister G. wouldn't give up on him. It isn't his way to throw in the towel when some living thing depends on him. In the midst of his struggles with the tiny, weak little chicken, the boys arrived.

All their sympathies went out immediately to the little invalid who was gasping out his last breaths in a coop alone, served, tended and nursed by Mister G. and his grandsons. Around the clock one of the four hovered over the small chicken. "When it dies, what'll I say?" I wondered.

I had had one experience trying to explain death to a young child. These grandsons' mother had had a bowl of goldfish — poor little city tyke — at their age. One of the fish had turned up its toes, floated dead and disconsolate on top the water. I think she overfed it. "Do something," she had commanded me, "*do* something, Mother!"

It was the first breach of perfect faith. Until then, Mother was omnipotent. But I could do nothing. The fish was totally, coldly, and heartbreakingly dead. With stoical but disillusioned control she had finally flushed the dead fish down the toilet, which is the only way I know of to dispose of dead goldfish in the city. But never again did she believe Mother could do all things. Mother was supposed to be wholly wise and wholly powerful. But Mother had let her fish die.

Well, I didn't hanker for the blame of this chicken's death.

I learned, quickly, that there is a world of difference between little girls and little boys. As long as that sick chicken lived my daughter's sons hovered over it in utter absorption and concern. Nothing was too much trouble or too difficult for them to do for it. But when it died, as it did, they were abominably full of glee. "Now! Now, we can have a funeral!" Not a tear did they waste, nor a second.

They demanded a coffin, so I unearthed a shoebox and lined it with Kleenex. They bore it away and we heard nothing more for a couple of hours. Then they descended upon us. "Where are our good clothes? Where is the bathtub? Where are our white shirts? Where are our ties? Where's the comb . . . and the toothbrush . . . and our jockshorts?"

Eventually everybody got bathed and jockshorted and whiteshirted and toothbrushed and blacktied and haircombed. We must all, everybody, come to the funeral.

A small ditch had been dug. It had also been lined with grass and flowers. To one side lay the shoebox with the tiny emaciated little skeleton of the small dead chicken in it. We gathered around it. With all the dignity of an ordained parson Bart instructed us. "Join hands," he said.

We joined hands.

"Now we have to pray," he said.

We waited.

We waited interminably until Scott's little pipsqueak voice suddenly found the courage to intone, "Come, Lord Jesus, be our guest. Let this food by Thee be blest."

It was the first table grace their mother had been taught which, in turn, she had passed on to them. Startled, Mister G. and I yet contained ourselves.

"Now," Bart said, "we'll sing."

We sang.

Mister G. would not be a proper Kentucky ridgerunner if he didn't pick a mean guitar and have an endless repertoire of hillbilly, cowboy, and Bible belt gospel songs. My daughter's sons knew hundreds of them. Every night after supper, if there wasn't a theatrical production, there was a sing on the front porch. Mister G.'s guitar and his offbeat repertoire were always prominent.

At Bart's behest we now stood around the slit trench and sang, but what we sang was no funeral hymn. Apparently not knowing a religious song from any other, he raised his voice and led us through all six verses of his favorite cowboy song. "Come along boys and listen to my tale, I'll tell you 'bout my troubles on the old Chisholm Trail, come a ki-yi-yippee-yippee-ay, yippee-ay, come-a-ki-yi-yippee-yippee-ay!"

No chicken was ever buried in more style.

At the end, we solemnly knelt while Bart laid the little dead thing to rest, quoting the scripture ponderously, "Ashes to ashes and dust to dust." Then we sprinkled the dust of the big farm on the small grave.

The rites finished we still waited. Bart rose from his knees, dusted the earth from them, and spread his hands. "That's all. Last one in the house is a rotten egg."

There is no doubt who were the two rotten eggs!

One of the nicest things that came out of those summer "sings" on the front porch was that we learned Bart was rather gifted musically. All the boys sang well, all had a fine

sense of rhythm, but Bart began early, at seven as I recall, to
finger Mister G.'s guitar and make musical sense on it. Mister
G. taught him a few simple chords and within a year or two
it was Bart who had the guitar when we sang. We gave him
his first small-size guitar when he was nine, that summer of
1957, and it was that summer that they, with Mister G.,
branched into composing! I quote here from Mister G.'s
column "Spout Springs Splashes" written shortly after the
event:

Highly artistic talents of a musical nature too long sup-
pressed have at last burst forth upon an unsuspecting world
from the Hollow here. The Hancock boys and I have written
a song. Possibly because we have never attempted anything
on such a high plane as song writing, this didn't come easily;
it required two evenings of the hardest thinking to complete
the final draft. And here is our song:

TWILIGHT IN THE HOLLOW
by the Hancocks
(Tune by H.G.)

I

When it's twilight in the Hollow,
When the sun goes down each day;
We will watch the darting swallow,
On the evening breezes play.

1st Chorus:

There's an evening star and a whippoorwill
And a lot of frogs a-callin',
A cricket in a thicket and an owl on the hill,
And the neighbors' cows a-bawlin'.

II

When it's night time in the Hollow,
When the moon shines brightly down,
Then the friendly fireflies follow,
Like a southwind without sound.

2nd Chorus:

There's a moonbeam caught in a sycamore tree,
And a mockingbird a-singin';
There's a minnow in the middle of a puddle in the creek,
And a hound dog's howl a-ringin'.

(Not to be picked or sung without permission!)

The swallow flew into the song of its own accord. Scott threw in the cricket and the minnow. Mike caught the fireflies and Bart hung the moon. Janice supplied the moonbeam and sycamore tree and I led in the hound. This was all done in the manner of ad men selecting a new slogan for soap or lipstick, all of us saying anything that came to mind, then editing down to the final draft. The tune is like nothing ever heard before and it can be seen the choruses and verses are not of the same tempo. The verses are ballad style and the choruses rock a little. While we were being creative we thought we might as well go the whole hog and create something really original. It can't be said of us we follow the beaten track.

Bart's equipment now, five years later, is all electrical and he long ago left Mister G. way behind. We sing just as much, but Mister G. takes the rhythm now while it's Bart's guitar that leads and often goes soaring into a picking and stringing so intricate Mister G. just shakes his head. Bart's love is wholly folk guitar and while he was mastering the instrument he was influenced considerably and inevitably by the records to which he listened constantly. He has begun, however, to make his own arrangements, develop his own style, and to experiment more freely.

He is a rangy boy, at fourteen topping me by half a foot, and sometimes watching him bent over his guitar, working on some special phrasing, so intent as to be unaware of where he is, I am flooded by the same strong love I had for his mother at that age and the same yearning feeling of God keep him and a bursting gratitude that the "favoritest grandfather in the *whole, wide* world" taught him something which will give him pleasure and joy all his life.

Life with these boys has not always run evenly and been wholly joyous. They've come croppers, been seriously ill, broken their share of bones, got their share of teeth knocked out, had their share of being lanced, needled, stitched and patched. Often I have wondered how their mother has managed not to turn gray by now. But I suppose when you live in the eye of a hurricane you get used to being blown with the wind. She doesn't panic easily. If a boy chops a finger half off she thrusts an aspirin down his throat to ease the pain, holds the finger together with a bandage, and hauls him to the doctor for proper stitching up, all the while keeping his mind off his injury with a running, laughing patter.

She never shudders over what might have happened. She just says thank God it didn't. And she doesn't forbid further experiments. She takes reasonable precautions and makes sensible safety rules but if things go awry nonetheless, they just go awry. Boys have got to learn to handle hatchets and hammers and saws and they've got to mash fingers and cut them, climb trees and break bones, get bloody noses and black eyes.

Nothing dreadful has happened to them, although there have been some heartstopping scares. They climbed, all of them, before they could walk, and by the time all three were toddling the only real way to insure their safety would have been to padlock everything that would open or pull out. Almost the first thing they learned to do was to use cupboard drawers as stairsteps, or the refrigerator shelves, or any piece of furniture that could be dragged near a larger one. They got some bumps and there was some destruction, but nothing catastrophic.

But now, this summer of 1957, they were big boys, six, eight and nine. They could be expected to understand when told no, and to obey. And they were also big enough to line up and give a little taste of hickory tea if they didn't obey. We could expect poison ivy, some cuts and bruises and stings, but they were normal. We laid in our usual supply of band-aids, poison ivy lotion, children's aspirins, a big box of soda for stings and burns, and new snakebite kit. That done, we lumped snakes with hammers, saws, and hatchets, and hoped for the best.

We could talk of little else, naturally, except the new house we were going to build. The boys were vastly interested. They thought a log house was simply the most — downright larky. Mister G.'s cousin, Edgar, had already begun taking down the log sets we had bought and as day after day passed bringing more and more truckloads of logs their excitement mounted.

It was our intention to keep each set of logs separate and

Mister G. had allocated space for each — to the right, to the left, before and behind. As the stacks mounted we came slowly to be fenced in by these stacks. From whatever point we looked out, all we could see was logs. Then the stones from the various chimneys we had bought began to turn up. And the beams and the old poplar siding from the little frame house. All these piles of stuff provided fascinating places to play and they became submarines, destroyers, battleships, even the *Kon-tiki,* forts to defend or attack. Mister G. and I thought we were being right orderly with it all. We knew where it was going pretty soon and nearly everything was near its eventual destination.

We were disillusioned when we overheard Scott tell a neighbor lad one day, "It's gonna be one of those do-it-yourself jobs." He paused, looked around, then added thoughtfully, "I sure hope they know *how* to do it. It's nothing but a big mess right now."

Chapter 7
Mister G. Takes the Floor

My Mrs. G. has a lot of misconceptions about how this old house got built. I haven't seen fit to disillusion her before but there is no better time than the present. Actually, she has only the vaguest idea how it was done. She knew to the last chimney rock and shingle what she wanted but only three men know how she got it, myself, my cousin Edgar Giles, and our neighbor, Joe Spires. And she doesn't know what miracles were passed for us to do it.

In the Bible we are told the Lord said, Let there be thus and so, and it came to pass. Let there be daylight and darkness, He said, and it happened. Let there be mountains and seas and fishes and animals, He decreed, and there were. But if He could have had the assistance of my Mrs. G. — a first class idea girl — a lot of other things would have come to pass which would have made life on this planet more pleasant. Back in those days they wouldn't have cost so much either.

Mrs. G. would have had very positive ideas about what to "let there be." As, for instance, let there be little streams of water running up- and downhill across ridges and through our yards as we wanted them. Let there be evergreen maples, sycamores and rosebushes around our houses at all times. Let there be seashores in our back yards, and in the rivers let there be fishes which don't smell and taste so fishy, and without bones. Oh, she could have made life so much more beautiful. I'm truly sorry she didn't have a hand in the creation of our earth, at its beginning, when all that was necessary to say was let there be and it came to pass.

Even at this late date, however, Mrs. G. has a knack for saying let there be. It takes me and a lot of money, but when Mrs. G. says let there be, it usually does come to pass. We bought this Spout Springs place because water won't run uphill the way she wanted it to do when we lived on the ridge. "Let us have a house with water running nearby," she said, and it came to pass.

Then she said, "Let us have a house with a roof of hand-rived shingles." And it happened.

"Let us have a *big* house," she said, "made of logs, forty-two feet east to west, fifty-six feet north to south. Let there be running water in it, and a modern sewage system. Let there be timber cut from our own woods for the middle part not built of logs. Let there be a door here and a window there. Let there be a big chimney on the east end and a well at the northwest corner. Let there be heavy hand-hewn beams to support ceilings nine feet high. Let there be hand-sanded kitchen cupboards and bookshelves and above all let there be room for many visitors." And it has all come to pass.

She puts it differently. She says, "Where there's a will, there's a way." But it amounts to the same thing for while she has the will it's usually up to me to find the way.

Not always.

Mrs. G. said, "Let there be books in libraries and on book-shelves which I have written," and that, too, came to pass. And when her life was threatened by cancer she said, "Let there be no fear," and for both of us there was as little as is humanly possible. Sometimes when Mrs. G. says let there be, it's a very comforting thing.

But now she was saying let there be a big house built here among these trees on the bank of Spout Springs Branch, and she sat down with half the stock of cardboard in the store-room of the *Adair County News* to draw plans.

But that wasn't where I began.

There were so many things to do before we'd need that plan of hers that I went around for a week trying to decide what to do first. We were living in the little cottage that came with the place. Obviously we had to get out of it, for obviously it had to come down before we could begin put-ting up the log house. But where were we going to live? "Oh, we can just camp out somewhere," Mrs. G. said airily, "just so it has a roof and four walls."

Now, I know my Mrs. G. a lot better than that. She can camp out for a month, or maybe two months or even three, without squawking. She's hardy and tough and she might even enjoy it for a while. But she would no more be willing to camp out for a year, and I figured it would take a year at the minimum for us to build this dream castle of hers, than she would be willing to go without food. She was going to need a lot more than a roof and four walls.

After I'd found someplace for us to live, I'd have to find somebody to move us. Here in the country you don't just pick up the telephone and call the movers. To begin with, the telephone company hasn't discovered anybody lives back in these hills and there is no telephone service. Second, there are no movers. None that is, nearer than Louisville, which is a hundred miles north of us.

All right, I said to myself. Get us a place to live and get us moved. Then tear down the cottage. Then tear down the fishing camp and move it. Then traipse all over Adair County for more logs. Then find . . . then pay . . . then do . . . then go nuts!

What I actually did first when I understood once and for all there would be no budging from that decree of Mrs. G.'s for a log house was to make a trip to Lebanon forty miles away for some beer. Our county is dry by local option, but just forty miles north of us alcoholic spirits flow freely. I wanted enough beer to last me the duration. I thought I'd need every drop of it.

That night, somewhat solaced, I looked at Mrs. G.'s blueprint and listened to her explanations — doors here, windows there, rooms that even on her quarter-inch scale looked enormous, electrical outlets (eight, no less, to every room!), wall heights, widths, the works. It made me desperate enough to ask, "Why do you want all that space? Why must it be so big? There are just two of us!"

"For people," she said in genuine astonishment, "for the grandsons, and the bachelors, and our families, and for friends!"

That, too, has come to pass. There have been times when I have wondered if we didn't build Spout Springs House for everybody but ourselves. Times when I've wondered if perhaps everybody we knew didn't think of it as a hotel or roadhouse or tavern. Times when, during the tourist season and the strange cars are sometimes parked six deep, I am seriously tempted to put up a sign: Entrance fee . . . 50¢ for adults, 25¢ for children. Full tour, $1.00.

But I don't. I just take to my heels and the woods if I spot the tourists in time.

I continued to study the blueprint.

There was a long silence. It was broken when Mrs. G. said, "How long does it take green moss to grow on a shingle roof?"

That has not yet come to pass. Mrs. G. has not yet been able to accomplish it nor have I been able to accomplish it for her. Green moss grows where it pleases, and our shingle roof apparently is not where it pleases. But don't think I don't take a quick look every time I come up the drive. It can happen yet.

I couldn't sleep for a long time that night. My mind was whizzing with all the things that needed to be done and all at the same time. No man could possibly do them all! Like a bolt of lightning it hit me then. I got up and found a pad of paper and a pencil and in strong, positive, underlined words, I wrote what *had* to be done first:

1. *GET HELP!!*

I slept like one of Mrs. G.'s dratted logs the rest of the night.

The next morning I expanded that little item. See Cousin Edgar, I wrote, about taking down and moving the fishing camp. See William Payne about using his truck and all his kinfolks to move *us*. See Johnny Mings about renting us his house. See George Spires about helping me tear down the cottage. I might, I thought, be tilting at windmills but at least I was astride my horse and had him headed in one direction — forward.

A noble quality of us ridgerunners, defined by our eminent *Courier-Journal* columnist, Allan Trout, as a man who does the best he can according to his lights, is that of ingenuity. Most of us in the north end of Adair County have had to scrabble a hard living and most of us have learned to do a little bit of everything and do it passing well. Some of us do one thing better than others, but pool our combined resources and we are pretty dauntless. Take Mrs. G.'s will, add the brains and brawn of half a dozen ridgerunners, and a little fatter bank account than we were used to, and "can do" came up the answer.

Cousin Edgar proved agreeable. He contracted to take down the fishing camp, rock chimney and all, and move it to Spout Springs. I wanted no part of that job. I was going to have my hands full putting it back together again.

Cousin Edgar wasted no time. I made him my proposition as he ate his breakfast shortly after daybreak and when I left he was throwing mauls and sledgehammers and saws and crowbars into the back of his car. He meant to begin at once.

Being in the neighborhood, I went on to see George Spires. We had bought the Spout Springs farm from his father. The house I was going to ask him to help me tear down had been his home. In fact, he was born in it and had never lived in another. Didn't seem to bother him. He agreed to help us and he was ready to begin at once, too. But Mrs. G. had to be moved first. She was already up to her ears with our three grandsons on a visit and a short story that wouldn't come right. I didn't think she would appreciate having the house torn down around her head too.

But it was a day when all things went well. I made a quick sashay to Campbellsville where Johnny Mings was now living. "Sure," he said, "you can have the farmhouse. Only thing is, Fanny's got some things stored upstairs. If you're aiming to use the upstairs we'll have to move 'em."

"How many rooms downstairs?" I asked.

"Five," he said.

"Plenty," I told him. "Leave Miss Fanny's things alone."

Next I tackled William Payne who had a five-ton truck and scads of relatives. "Just let me know when you want me," he said.

"Tomorrow," I said unthinkingly.

Have you ever seen a woman get ready to move on twelve hours notice? Things fly, I can tell you. And some of them aren't too well aimed!

My Mrs. G. is an auction hound and over the years she had managed to acquire a house full of some of the biggest and heaviest pieces of furniture ever made. Especially an old upright piano, an eight-foot sofa, three marble-topped chests, a Spanish mission oak dining table and dish cabinet, chairs that three people could sit in at the same time, and so on. I warned William Payne and he brought six strong-backed men with him, with the happy result that I could wander around directing the proceedings with a can of beer in my hand. It was one of the best moving days I ever had.

I wondered why I hadn't thought of this business of getting help much earlier in my life. It was Somerset Maugham who said, I believe, "I never do anything for myself I can pay somebody else to do for me." I like the sound of that but sadly I knew it was going to have short shrift with me. Next morning George and I were going to begin tearing down his old home.

If you've never had to tear down a house and clean up the mess to build another on the same spot, rejoice. It shouldn't happen to anybody. The cottage had been built of hardwoods — oak, beech, hickory — while still green. It had been built many years before and was well seasoned by now. There was no use trying to save anything except the metal roofing and a few of the better doors and windows. The only way we could get that house down was to wreck it.

There's nothing dramatic about taking down an old house, except that it defies you. George's father had built permanently. For a week we fought it. Each day Edgar's old truck rolled up with another load of logs and rocks. Having contracted to take down the fishing camp for a set fee he had felt prosperous enough to hire some help himself and he was working a lot faster than George and I were. He brought the last load in the day we finally got the metal roof off the cottage. I wrote him a check and promptly propositioned him to pitch in on the cottage with us. He grinned and agreed and I heaved a long sigh. Maybe Edgar knew a better way to wreck an old house than I did.

I hold just one thing against my cousin Edgar. He didn't catch my high sign on the day Mrs. G. explained to him that we needed two or three more sets of logs for the house.

I was still harboring hopes of talking her out of building the entire house of logs. It would have been a lot simpler to

use the fishing camp for one big log room and make the rest
of the house out of something more sensible, such as lumber,
for instance. But as she burbled on Edgar caught the spirit
and volunteered the unnecessary information that he knew
of one log house that could be bought. He was sure of that
because it belonged to a relative of his wife. I wiggled my
eyebrows and shuffled my feet and all but stood on my head
to catch his eye but he was as long gone as she was. "There's
another one the other side of Columbia," he rambled on.
"Fellow uses it for a barn. Looks to be a big one." And he
thought he could put his hands on two or three more. I could
have put my hands around his throat and squeezed tight right
then. It was beginning to look as though Edgar wasn't on
my side.

I'm sunk, I told myself as I slunk away. I'm stuck with
putting up this log castle.

One hope still stayed with me. The logs might be priced
out of all reason. In that case perhaps Mrs. G.'s practical side,
and she has one though she doesn't often show it, might over-
come her deepest yearnings. I meant to press that advantage
home. I didn't have a ghost of a chance. The logs were so
cheap it was ridiculous and sickening. And old chimneys
came with every one of them. In black and white, as plain
as the nose on your face, my fate was sealed. Mrs. G. chortled
and I groaned but there was no escaping the fact that we
could build a log house as big as she wanted for about half
what the same house would cost in lumber and for about one-
fourth what it would cost in brick. I was doomed to hustle
logs and rocks for the next twelve months.

Mrs. G. has never been unkind enough to say out loud that
she thinks I'm lazy but she has come close enough for me to
protest I'm not lazy, I'm just thrifty with my energies. I

don't know what I'm saving them for but they'll come in handy some day and I don't want to be caught short. Now, she was planning to be the wildest kind of spendthrift with them.

In fact, she sailed right up to the clouds. Since logs were so cheap we could expand the house. It could now become a really *big* house! Mrs. G. zoomed into high gear with a new blueprint which, when shown to me, seemed to have the proportions of a landing strip with parade ground attached. "The house can sort of ramble," she said, explaining, "just so you miss the trees. Here and here and here."

To my flabbergasted horror she had rooms *around* trees, *between* trees, and *under* trees, with bathrooms at either end and the kitchen in the middle. The plumbing system alone would have been a nightmare and I was already having plenty of those with her first blueprint.

I don't often put my foot down with my lady. It wouldn't often do any good, for she has a way of making me take it right back up again. But this time I put it down good and hard and I kept it down. "We'll stick to the first plan," I said.

"But why?"

"Because I say so."

She didn't forgive me until we spent our first winter in the new house. Then she discovered it cost one hundred dollars a month to heat what we had built. It made her shudder to think what it would have cost to heat the one she really wanted.

Mrs. G. still thinks, however, the house was built around the trees. Joe Spires and I know better. It was built around the plumbing system. The toilet, to be specific.

Chapter 8
A Little Better than Plumb

WE FINALLY battered the cottage to the ground and then, leaving George to make what order he could of the mess scattered about, Mrs. G., Edgar, and I went in search of logs.

I will skip lightly over that ordeal, for I don't even like to remember it. It is sufficient to say that the dog days were upon us and I felt all too much like a dog myself — hot, uninspired, harried and hopeless. By September we had found and bought three sets of logs to add to the fishing camp and a poplar-framed cabin which a great-uncle of mine had built around 1849. Mrs. G. couldn't resist it because of the hand-planed boarding, the big axed kitchen beams, and a winding corner stairway which, in her ignorance, she thought could be lifted out bodily and put somewhere in the new house.

Edgar took on the job of taking down all the houses we had bought and moving them. I had now to face up to what I had been pushing to the back of my mind all summer — the plumbing system. It had to be laid out and the groundwork done before the first rock or log was put in place.

Once upon a time, before Spout Springs, I had put in a complete water system in a house already built. To the best of my knowledge it's still working, but I didn't want to put in another system any such way. The business of lying on my belly under a house and working with a shovel just plain didn't appeal to me. Besides, if I had found it hard to do ten years earlier, my growing paunch would have made it impossible now. So, I told myself, bracing back as manfully as the paunch would allow, come to grips with it my lad and get on with the job.

I had a few wild ideas before coming to grips with it, however. Such as installing all the fixtures in some attic space and letting the forces of gravity do the work. But it was hard to imagine Mrs. G. going upstairs to wash dishes, peel potatoes, or commune with nature, so that notion died aborning.

I am not a plumber. When I rigged up that first water system I had a book to guide me and what I couldn't understand I skipped and just followed my nose. The book had long since been mislaid but I remembered enough of it to know that where Mrs. G. saw bright, shining bathroom fixtures and a double-barreled sink, with hot and cold running water from all spigots, there must be numberless joints of tile, two lines of pipes, thousands of connections and washers, ventilators, and ditches. Hundreds of feet of ditches!

The house is built in the shape of a slightly inebriated T.

On the south, running east and west, is the top of the T. Here are the living room and bedroom, 42 x 18 feet overall. Immediately north and adjoining is a 20 x 20 foot section, not made of logs, in which are the bathroom, entrance hall, study, and dining room. The kitchen, of logs, is 18 x 20 feet and attached to the middle section. And a pumproom measuring 10 x 14 is attached to the west of the kitchen.

Surrounding the house were: east, a giant sycamore, maple and box elder. North, a peach tree and an American hornbeam. The trigonometrical angles and distances between all those trees I don't know, but it wasn't enough. Never was. And besides all the immovable trees surrounding the house there had to be allowances made for certain rosebushes, flowering annuals and herb beds which George's mother had planted and Mrs. G. wanted to keep. And an old well.

Now, midst the trees and other obstacles I had to fit a house of given dimensions and put in it a sewage system that would work, and fit fixtures in according to Mrs. G.'s blueprint. I had to think in terms of inches, feet, yards, tree roots, rosebushes and sweet basil! It took another trip to Lebanon and another case of beer to find the courage to begin.

The edge of horror taken off, I tackled it.

First, I had to figure out lines for the sewage system. I didn't want all the refuse to be piped into the septic tank so there had to be two outlets, one for the toilet and one for all the other fixtures.

With dimensions in hand I took up my position at the toilet location. It was the focal point. For several days I stood like a bird dog on point, plotting out the sewer lines. Surrounded by piles of logs and mountains of chimney rocks, I imagined myself at the base of a giant V. Down the right prong ran the line to the septic tank. Directionwise that wasn't such a problem. It missed all the more important trees and shrubs and disappeared southward over the horizon. But the line to drain water wastes was something else again. It ran dead center through the big maple tree in the front yard. That wouldn't work. But to bend it either right or left would run it through the root system of either the sycamore or the box elder. That wouldn't do, either. And if I moved the whole system, house and all, far enough *south* to miss all the trees in front, there would be a big sycamore in the southeast quarter of the bedroom. I never thought I'd like a sycamore in the bedroom.

If the entire plan was moved far enough *north* to miss the root systems, the house would be completely out from under the shade trees and the septic tank would have to be buried under Ancil Spires's corncrib. I didn't think *he* would appreciate that.

How I finally worked it out sounds highly improbable and a little unintelligible. I drove a stake at the toilet site and one at the approximate location of the kitchen sink. Straight east from the sink the line ran through only a few tree roots. So. The basin-bath line no longer made the left prong of the giant V mark. Instead it made a complete right angle, ran uphill, and connected with the sink!

Running a line uphill was what I had been trying to get away from. It's something you just don't do. Besides the vacuum, I think the only other thing nature abhors must be a sewer line running upstream. But I had to do it. The amazing thing is, it works.

After checking the lie of the land I found it didn't amount to much after all. The house site was almost level. In fact, when I began figuring how deep to dig the ditches for the pipelines I found it was a little better than level. And there is such a thing as being a little bit better than level or plumb. Of course my carpenter books don't say so, but neither do they say there is *no* such thing. Joe Spires is my authority.

Joe does fine carpentry work and a lot of it. He and his helper were putting up some studding once which had to be exactly plumb. He told his helper so. While the helper held the spirit level to the stud Joe nailed it securely in place. Finished, he asked, "Are you sure it was plumb, Ab?"

"Sure was," Ab rejoined cheerfully. "Fact is, Joe, hit was jist a little bit better'n plumb 'ccordin' to the level."

Joe checked for himself and sure enough it was — a little better than plumb.

I discovered our house site was a little better than level after I ordered an eye level to use in determining how deep to dig the sewer lines.

Taking my old familiar stance at the toilet site again I had George hold a rod while I sighted and figured, sighted and figured. My old plumbing book had said that the drop per foot in a sewer line should not be less than one-eighth of an inch nor more than one-quarter of an inch. I split the difference and dropped mine three-sixteenths of an inch to the foot. So, with that drop rate, a ditch eighty feet long *should* have been only fifteen inches deep if the ground were perfectly level. Less if it were sloping away, which it looked to be. You think it turned out that way? Eighty feet from the house we were digging waist deep! That's when I learned our house site was a little better than level no matter what the eye told you.

We have since discovered also that many of our walls are a bit better than plumb and most of our corners are something more than square. And some of our floors are better than level, too. But considering the lie of the land that's all to be expected, I imagine.

Now came three simultaneous digging jobs — two sewer lines and a new well.

There was a good well on the place already but it was tainted with iron. So tainted in fact that Mrs. G. took one look at its rusty color and shuddered to think what it would do to her nylon underwear and her good table linens. There must be a new well, she said.

"You'll have the same problem with a new well," I warned her. "Forty feet down you're going to hit iron water."

"Then for goodness' sake don't go forty feet!"

I stared at her. "What kind of well do you have in mind?"

"Just a hole in the ground with water in it."

When I could speak, I said, "You *know* you've got to drill at least a hundred feet to find pure water."

"No, you don't. You've just got to have a husband who was in the Corps of Engineers five years and can purify ditch water if necessary."

I took a deep breath. "Let me get this clear. This is to be a shallow well. Just an old-fashioned hand-dug, round well. Is that right?"

"That's right. Just an old-fashioned big hole in the ground."

"It'll be done, ma'am," I said.

And it was. But it was done a little sooner than I expected and gave a little more trouble than I wanted.

By now, "get help" had become a rule of thumb with me. So I got all the help I could find for all this digging, about twenty teen-age boys eventually.

They came and they dug and I think they all hit water,

both sewer lines and well, at about the same time and at the same exact depth — sixteen inches down!

There's nothing really wrong with the land in Spout Springs Hollow except that it's not land. It's perfectly good gravel underlaid with water at sixteen inches. A thick morning fog or a heavy dew will raise the water table considerably and after a rain boots must be worn. To sum up the condition, what looks like land here is like the Platte River, too thin to plow and too thick to drink. And wells and sewer lines were not meant to be dug in it nor houses built upon it.

When water began to gush up on all sides I scampered to borrow an irrigation pump and by some frantic maneuvering managed to keep ditches and well at least squashily dry while digging proceeded to the required depth — twenty feet for the well and whatever it took for the sewer lines.

We never got twenty feet for the well. At fourteen feet the boys tapped an underground spring and *two* irrigation pumps working furiously round the clock couldn't handle the outflow of water. Wearily we called it a day. I said, that's it, boys, and we tiled it, closed it up, cemented a top over it, placed a shallow-well electric pump handy and you know something? That water hasn't had to be purified to this hour. It's the sweetest, cleanest, purest, best water that ever ran any household and as soft as rain from the heavens. That well is a feather in Mrs. G.'s cap. When everybody else is practicing thrift with water during a long droughty season, Mrs. G. could still operate an automatic laundry and never miss a drop. I had mourned because we couldn't tap the big Spout Spring itself and pipe it a quarter of a mile into the house. I know it's pure coincidence we hit one in our own back yard but when I consider it seriously it gives me goosebumps. My lady's instincts are too often near the miraculous for my comfort.

Nothing else was standing still while sewer lines and the well were being dug. Oh, my, no! So many other things were going on that if I needed six hands and two more sets of brains to keep abreast at the time, the art of writing would have to develop a new dimension to deal adequately with them now.

To simplify, you may assume that the sewer lines and the well got dug. I had now to lay out Mrs. G.'s houseplan on

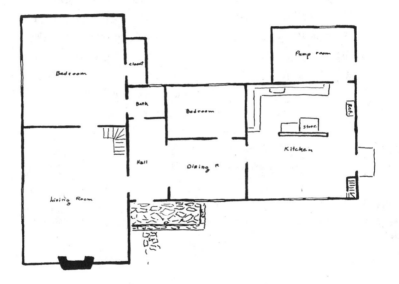

the most solid ground to be found and yet avoid the "dreen" in back, the trees on all sides, and the creek in front. It wasn't easy. This was the situation:

As can be seen, I was caught between a rock and a hard place and if anybody thinks I could have cut down the sycamore or the box elder he couldn't be more wrong. I hinted at cutting the box elder once, but only once. Such a howl of anguish went up that I preferred to cope with anything rather than hear it again.

The trouble with Mrs. G. is that she is so good and so wonderful in so many ways, at the same time so trustingly naïve and ignorant of facts, that she gets to your heartstrings and you want her to have what she wants. Her husband does, at least. When she wails that trees *know* when they're being cut, that they *feel* pain, she goes orbiting off into ghostly unreality that leaves me behind, but if she is convinced of it, it would take more harshness than I possess to hurt *her* by cutting one of her trees.

I have tried patiently to understand my lady for a good many years, and give and take a little I have managed pretty well when I have only her to face. But when she is reinforced, as she occasionally is, by her close friend, Pansy Phillips, all I can do is make a hasty retreat and stuff my ears against their joined wails.

About the same time I hinted at cutting the box elder tree, I began a chore which I felt had needed doing since we bought the place, tearing down an old barn and some fencing. The barn was across the creek and slightly upstream from the house and it had been there forever — at least as far back as I could remember. One side had fallen in and the other was canted dangerously into the wind and the whole thing was covered in vines. The fence was a patched affair loaded down with more greenery. The barn was a menace to life and limb. It was held up by a few cross timbers and I was afraid one of the workmen would wander in, brush against one of the timbers and the whole thing would come down around his head. The vines on both the barn and the fence were the best hiding places for snakes I'd ever seen. I had felt considerable anxiety about the whole situation since work had started on the new house.

We were, of course, camping out in the cottage we had rented and Pansy was spending the day with Mrs. G. She visited frequently during the housebuilding and though I never heard her offer any advice she was in Mrs. G.'s confidence every log of the way and felt that if she didn't personally see how much progress had been made every week or so the whole project might fall in.

I had a half day's peace before they drove over from the cottage, and had the vines hacked down and the fencing laid low and a good part of the barn wrecked. Only one wall and half the roof was left and I was just about to pull the brace that would send that tumbling down when they came flying and yelping across the creek. "What are you *doing?* What have you *done?*"

It looked obvious to me. "I'm wrecking this old barn."

"But you can't! You can't!"

"I don't see why not. Anyway, I *have!*"

Rarely have I felt as bewildered as I did when I saw they were both actually in tears. They circled around that old heap of timbers and stones clutching their heads and moaning, picking up boards and pieces of vines. "It was so beautiful. It was so old, and the boards were so gray and weathered. And the old shingles had *moss* on them!" That was Mrs. G.

"And the trumpet vines were at least a hundred years old." That was Pansy. "Look at that main trunk. Look at the size of it! It takes at least a century to grow a trunk that size!"

"It covered the entire barn!"

"Some of these boards are chestnut!"

Pansy, who paints, suddenly put her hands on her hips. "Henry Giles, if it would do any good, I'd take a horsewhip to you! I didn't have a chance to paint this old barn. I didn't even have a chance to sketch it! And now it's gone. It's gone."

Well, there wasn't any arguing about that. It was gone all right. And there wasn't actually any point arguing about anything. No point in explaining. Once more I was up against this thing in my lady, vague and incomprehensible to me but about which she felt so strongly she could cry over it, and I thought the best thing I could do was creep away, put on sackcloth and ashes and perhaps go into the wilderness for forty days.

I was honestly mystified. There had been nothing beautiful about the old barn to me. What would have been beautiful to me, as a farmer, was a stout, sturdy, useful structure and a stout, sturdy, functional fence with clean fence rows.

Not until last year did I begin dimly to understand. Mrs. G. gave me for Christmas some oil paints, canvases and brushes and I began to dabble at painting. All at once it dawned on me that the lines of that old barn *had* been beautiful, sagged and caved and fallen in ruin, and that the covering vine had also been beautiful, and that the fence, patched and decrepit and weed- and vine-grown, had also been beautiful. I pondered my vandalism and wondered at my dullness. But it takes a long time to enrich ground made rocky and sterile by deprivation — and my childhood and youth were so poverty-ridden the years were nearly all deprivation. I won't live long enough to fill up all the empty places, but I try . . . I try. And if I could, I'd restore the old barn and the ancient trumpet vines. I'd like to paint them now, myself.

But, my problem that summer of 1957, was either to set the whole house back and build the bedroom on stilts over the "dreen" — a natural run-off of an ancient arm of the creek — which would have put the kitchen sink midway between a maple and a locust to say nothing of putting the toilet in the entrance hall, or I could set the house forward and build the chimney up through the limbs of the box elder tree. I chose to do it that way. As confused as I was, it somehow seemed simpler.

It turned out that when the rock chimney reached the box elder limbs I just took my old .22 rifle and some hollow-point bullets and kept the limbs shot off as Edgar and Joe went on up. A few months later I read that U.S. forest rangers had adopted that method of topping tall trees. Word of a good thing sure travels fast.

That decision made, George and I hauled off and drove ten thousand stakes around the foundation lines and stretched up several balls of twine between them.

I had expected, and planned, that the foundation would be built of concrete blocks set into a firm concrete footing. This was both sensible and simple and necessary, from my point of view, to carry the weight of the house and to reinforce the stress points. Mentioned to Mrs. G., the reaction was recoil. "Concrete blocks with a log house? Oh, that won't do!"

"What did you have in mind?"

"What the early settlers used. Rocks."

With great care and patience I explained that no early settler ever built a log house of such dimensions as ours, 52 x 42 feet, with its stress points crossing and recrossing. I refrained from adding that no early settler was that insane.

He threw up one log room, or at most two, and he didn't amble them around all over the place. Of course rock pillars were good enough to support his simple structure. I pointed out to my *esposa* that this would be one of the heaviest houses ever to raise its walls up to a roof line and that the foundation *had* to be strong.

"Can't you," she asked when she fully understood the problem, "make the footing of concrete, and all the pillars that don't show, then use rocks for the outer pillars that *do* show? But why aren't rocks just as strong as concrete?"

There was no getting around the fact that they are. But what I was trying to get around was the trouble. "You've *got* to have rocks, then?"

She was pretty miserable about it because she was beginning to grasp the idea of how formidable a job it would be to match up rocks to the precise level, but she was more miserable about concrete blocks showing. "No," she said finally, shaking her head in surrender, "do what you think best."

When she goes wistful like that, I melt. Concrete and concrete blocks would be used under the house at all stress points and where they would not show. Rock pillars and a rock outer hull could certainly give her what she wanted and there would be no weakness. But jumping Jehoshaphat, the extra work it would involve! So be it, however. My Mrs. G. was going to have her rock foundation — at least where it showed.

I'd hate to tell you what it finally cost in man hours and money. But it made her happy and it's always been my contention that money, any amount of it if you've got it, is a cheap price to pay for a woman's happiness.

All during this period Cousin Edgar was involved with

sorting through logs and rocks and lumber and other debris, marking it and piling it, scrapping and saving. So George and I began digging the foundation and pouring the concrete footing. There was no problem. We just dug until we hit water. In some places we hit water at six inches. In others, we dug fully as deep as sixteen. Wherever we hit it, we just poured concrete into the water.

While we were working with concrete we poured the foundations for the chimneys. At that time Mrs. G. wanted two, one in the living room, one in the kitchen. I thought one was a mistake on our tundra, and while I meant to try, I dreaded her eventual disappointment. All my life I had heard old-timers say you had to dig to solid rock for chimney foundations. Otherwise, they said, it would sink. Halfway to China we might have hit solid rock, but I doubt it. I am personally convinced this slush we live on comes out as mud in the Yangtze River.

Our friends the Sheldon Willocks built a fishing camp on the river many years ago. They have a massive chimney. Sheldon had its foundation dug to solid rock and it was sixteen feet down. It took three ordinary rock chimneys to bring the foundation up level with the ground before he could even begin to build the upper section.

Well, you do the best with what you've got. So we dug the chimney foundations down to water, twelve inches as I recall, and filled them up with concrete.

Even though I knew the chimneys would sink as fast as they were built, I carefully studied a government bulletin on how to build a good chimney and together Edgar and I figured out the measurements according to the chimney holes in the two ends of the house. I told Edgar we would get the proportions right even though we never had a chimney. I was convinced that as fast as rocks were laid they, and the foundation, would sink and keep right on sinking and we'd never get any higher than ground level. I hoped Mrs. G. would understand that there are *some* things that simply can't be done. But she was cheerfully certain that five tons of rock in each chimney would float on top the water.

And one of the most anguishing confessions I have ever had to make is that she was right. After the foundations were poured, but before work on the chimneys began, she changed her mind about the kitchen chimney. Decided to have another outside door instead. But that blasted stack of rocks which form the living room chimney has defied every known law of engineering as well as some not known before. Its foundation floats on water but it has never sunk that first fraction of an inch. For weeks I watched it for the first telltale cracks that would indicate it was sinking. Because I *knew* it was going to sink I kept hoping the cracks would show up early, before we got too far along with it. But stubbornly and against all theories of chimney building it refused to sink and it still, to this moment, stands there, solid and uncracked and unsunk. I am now convinced that if our world is destroyed by atomic missiles, hydrogen bombs, or whatever, that chimney will be the last landmark at Spout Springs to crumble and go down.

But my Mrs. G. would have been hung for a witch in Salem. She says let there be a well dug here and an everlasting spring of pure water is struck. She says let there be chimneys that float, and chimneys float. It gives one an eerie feeling to say the least.

When the concrete footings were hard we used the eye

level considerably as we built up the pillars of concrete blocks under the house and the rock pillars along the foundation line. George and Edgar would stack up some rocks then stand the "idiot" stick on top while I stood at the old familiar toilet location and jotted down readings. The toilet seat was about halfway between every two points in the house and was the only fixed position that could be used.

I needn't spell out the agony it was to find the right size and shape of rocks to make the pillars or what we had to do to level them off. In the event they weren't much more trouble than leveling concrete blocks. I made the mistake of digging the footings to water level, then bringing them to ground level with concrete. I thought it would be easier to level the pillars than to level the footings. I couldn't have been more wrong. But all was done eventually.

Now the sills and plates began to arrive.

Since Mrs. G. wanted everything homegrown if possible, we had cut whiteoak trees from our own timber for these sills and plates and Leonard Bryant had whipsawed them at his small mill. Some of these sills were eight feet long, some ten, some twelve, and four of them were twenty feet long. Two had to be twenty-two feet long. And all of them were eight inches square. It took the very last whiteoak tree on the place to make them all.

As a matter of fact, all the lumber for the middle section of the house was homegrown and, I might add, green and sappy and unseasoned. There were hundreds of 2 x 4 rafters, 2 x 6 floor joists, all the subflooring and boxing.

William Payne, who lives down the pike, had a chain saw and truck. He cut the timber and hauled the logs across the river to Leonard Bryant's mill. Then he hauled the sawed lumber to the house site. Both William and Leonard charged standard prices per thousand square feet for their work, but somewhere along the line something got out of control. I don't yet know how it was possible but using the timber off our own place cost us two dollars per board foot more than would the same amount of seasoned lumber from town!

But we haven't really regretted it. The good feeling we have when we look at that middle section and remember walking the woods to mark the trees to be cut more than repays us the extra cost. When the chips are down I have never regretted anything Mrs. G. whipsawed me into doing at the time. Though I thought she was asking the impossible, she wasn't, and every idea she had came up seven every time. She dreamed us and I built us a beautiful home.

Chapter 9
Board Trees and Shingle Boards

A GOOD PERCENTAGE of this house is creosote.

I wanted every piece to last from here to eternity, so to guard against termites and rotting every piece of lumber below the floor is creosoted. Sills, joists, braces, subflooring, all had their creosote bath. I kept the creosote factories running full blast during the building of the foundation and subfloor. Every place I went I'd pick up a few more jugs of creosote and I had all my friends bringing me what they could find. Buying creosote became such an obsession with me that I feared I could never find enough. And George did so much painting with it that it's still a mystery why he didn't come down with creosote poisoning. What I did was overbuy, of course, and every once in a while I still run across a spray can or unopened jug of creosote hiding behind a tree or in a clump of weeds or stashed behind something in an outbuilding.

At first I meant to creosote all the joints where the logs were connected, too. It was Mrs. G. who, watching me attack a corner with tar brush and bucket, said mildly, "Seems to me if those logs have stood a hundred and twenty-five years already without creosote they don't need it now."

The shock of it was like an electric current. Drowned in a creosote binge I hadn't thought of it but the reasoning was sensible, simple and true. I felt like any other man caught making an ass of himself and for a moment I just froze. Then with what I hoped was unruffled calm and poise I slowly laid down the tar brush, whistled a few bars of "Crawdad Hole" to show how nonchalant I was, hummed and hawed a time or two and said, judicially, "Don't know but what takin' 'em down and disturbin' 'em might have stirred up some nests. Termites are a funny kind of ant."

Mrs. G. walked away. But over her departing shoulder there floated back one more bit of wisdom. "Before you take all that trouble, why don't you look and see?"

One bucket of creosote was wasted right then. I couldn't resist kicking it as far as I could.

We didn't have a house-raising when we put up the log walls. For one thing there weren't enough men in Spout Springs, Neatsville and Pellyton combined to put them up in one day. For another there was too much figuring on angles and connections, too many new doors and windows to be cut out, too many old ones to be closed up and patched. Our walls had to be raised by blueprint and a little at a time.

By keeping 2 x 4 skids well oiled with creosote and using ropes and pulleys and prying poles, George and Edgar laid the logs to a greater height than you'd think possible for two men to do. But even they finally reached a limit. And I couldn't help because I had had to go back to newspapering.

I believe it was along about this time that Joe Spires got all of Indiana he could take and came home. He had been up there working for several months. Long before he had promised to help build our house, so now he kept his promise. He and his grown son, Donald, pitched in with George and Edgar and helped lay logs until they reached the top plates — those twenty and twenty-two foot 2 x 8's of green whiteoak that now had to be hoisted to the top of the logs. There, as Edgar put it, we had to have more "weak minds and strong backs."

I don't remember now how many helped with the top plates but it was a slew of men and boys and they got them into place in one day. I never asked how they did it. I was just grateful to have Mrs. G. report it had been done and nobody was hurt. One of those plates out of control could have killed half a dozen men.

The time had come, now, to pay off George. I would have hated it worse if he hadn't been going to a better job in Indiana. He was only sixteen years old but I never saw a better worker, nor a faster one. In an eight-hour day he only took thirty minutes off for lunch and he didn't waste one second of the rest of the time. You didn't have to show him or tell him what to do, either. I believe he was the most silent boy I ever was around, too. In two and a half months if he said more than a hundred words I don't remember them. He was all work and no play, too much so for my understanding but since it was to our advantage I didn't quarrel with it. In spite of his quietness we missed him a lot when he'd gone and will always wish him well. A lot of George got built into our house.

I felt considerably relieved to have Joe Spires on the job, however. He was the best carpenter in Adair County, and I felt nothing much could go wrong with our house with him and Edgar in charge. Quickly the roof braces and rafters went up and we were ready to lay on the shingleboards.

When Mrs. G. had said there must be a hand-rived shingle roof, it had posed something of a problem. Vaguely I knew we had to begin with what old-timers call "board trees," but the days when you could go out and chop down one of these monsters have long been over in our parts. Over the years, and with but few exceptions, every log big enough to saw out enough lumber to make a box of matches has been cut.

However, after word got out that we were looking for some board trees we started hearing about such trees scattered around over the county that *might* be bought. I checked out some of the rumors and usually it turned out there was only one such tree, or two at the most, and usually the owner had plans of his own — such as building a barn or adding a room to his home. There seemed to be no answer to the board tree problem until I mentioned it to Joe. Joe said, "See Billy Joe Breeding. If there's any board timber left, it's probably on Billy Joe's place."

All my life I had hunted squirrels and dug ginseng in the upland part of the Breeding farm but I had never kept an eye out for board trees. After Joe suggested it, I took an afternoon to ramble through Billy Joe's woods. The trees were there, all right. Plenty of them. From my dad I had found out what to look for in a board tree. The bark should run straight up the trunk, not twine around like a vine. The tree should be white or red oak and it should be big, at least thirty inches in diameter, for several feet up the trunk and it should not have knot holes or limbs near the ground. Such a tree, according to my dad, ought to work up pretty good.

Billy Joe's woods were full of such trees but I wasn't sure he would sell them. As Joe Spires said, however, it wouldn't cost anything to ask. So, I went to see Billy Joe. "Sure," he said, "I'll let you have enough for your roof — if they're there."

I already knew they were there, and the beauty of it was that they were right at home. Billy Joe's place joins ours on the east, and immediately on top of the hill were those big, beautiful trees. That settled, all I had to do was figure out how many trees it would take to make enough shingle-boards to cover our house. Because he had been kind enough to turn me loose in his woods I sure didn't want to overdo it and cut more trees than we needed for the boards.

In math, I've studied unknown quantities which could be worked out with given formulas. But in figuring how many trees it would take to make all those boards, there was no formula. In the first place, I had no idea how many boards we needed. Roughly our house covers sixteen hundred square feet of ground. But the roof, being slanted as roofs generally are, was more than that. How much more was the problem.

I finally came up with a round figure, two thousand square feet of roof space to be covered with boards — *shingle* fashion! If I take leave of you right here and seem to soar into outer space it's because there is a world of difference between shingling a roof and shingleboarding a roof! Bought shingles may be any length and width and are put on lapped. Shingle-boards are two feet long and only four inches wide. On barns they are lapped only enough to nail together. On our house they had to be lapped like shingles so that only eight inches of the board could be seen, and no nail heads showing. If you have followed me this far you will know that you end up with a roof that is triple thick — practically indestructible and almost wholly leakproof. But how many boards to cover our house? Who could tell? How many ants are there in an ant-hill? How many bees in a hive? Or minnows in the branch?

I asked my dad how many it would take. I asked Ancil Spires how many. I asked Edgar and Joe. Hard to tell, they said. And my dad and Ancil Spires have probably nailed more boards in their lifetimes than any other two men in the county. In 1918 my dad covered a barn with boards. Last spring the barn fell down but the old roof was still good and turned water. But in Dad's and Ancil's board-roofing days they had their own timber, so if two trees didn't make enough boards to cover a building they just went out and cut two or three more. How many was never any problem for them.

Figures I didn't have and couldn't come up with. I went to Billy Joe and explained it. He said he understood. He said, "Cut what you think is enough and if it isn't, cut some more."

On a guess, I went through his woods and marked eight big oaks to cut. Then one day William Payne took his chain saw up on the hill and began cutting. With a team of horses Dillard White snaked the big logs to the top of the hill, dumped them over, then snaked them down a short hollow to a place where William could load them on his truck. The first logs of each tree were hauled out to my dad's, where William sawed them into two-foot cuts. The rest of the logs were sawed into lumber.

The two-foot cuts had to be split into "bolts" before boards could be rived. This is done by two men, one with a poleax, the other swinging a big maul made of hickory. Because I didn't know how to set the ax to make the cuts, I turned out to be the maul swinger. It's a muscle-building job, I suppose, but it's also pretty muscle tiring.

First the cut is split into halves, then quarters, and so on, down to the place a man who knows his business knows the bolt is small enough to handle with the froe. A froe is then used to rive the bolts into boards.

Now, let's go through the procedure for making one board.

Take one big oak tree, and I do mean big. Cut it down. Saw it into two-foot lengths. Turn one length up on its end. You'll need a man like my dad who knows how to split timber to set the ax and some less intelligent man like me to swing the maul. A good ax man can flick it loose and reset it quicker than you can raise your maul and swing it. You keep splitting until you're down to the heart wood which is thrown aside for the cook stove. You do this all day every day for all too many days, until you've got all your two-foot lengths from eight big trees split into bolts. Then you sit down and wipe your brow and watch a real old-timer work like lightning with his froe and rive out, one at a time but so fast they fall like rain, ten thousand shingle-boards which your lady wants to shelter her sweet head.

In our case it was my dad who rived out our shingles. Even if he hadn't been about the last man left to know how it was done, we wanted it that way. "Your dad's hand will have touched every board in our roof," Mrs. G. said, and I forgave her every hamstrung muscle in my arms and legs for her tenderness.

It is a beautiful operation to watch when a real craftsman has hold of the froe, and my dad is a real craftsman, deft, sure, and steady. In his prime he could drive out a thousand shingleboards a day and never raise a sweat. He's slowed down a little now. I don't suppose he did more than five hundred in any one day when he was working on ours. But we stood in awe of that.

The tools he used were all handmade and they looked something like this:

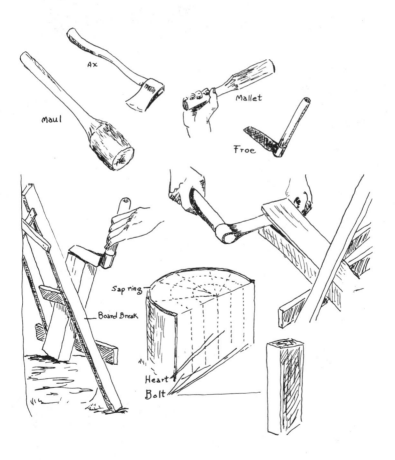

When he had finished we hauled the clean-smelling shingle-boards to our log house. You put them on green, for nails will split them if they're seasoned out. And if you're wise, you'll put them on in the dark of the moon!

Chapter 10
Floods and the Dark of the Moon

MISTER G. warned me that when the log walls were raised I might be disappointed. I wasn't, but I grant quickly that nothing looked less like a house. A barn, a very old and decrepit-looking barn, was a much better description of what we had. Logs for building are notched at the ends. They are laid then in overlapping and interlocking pattern. This leaves a wide space between which must be filled with "chinking." In the old days people chinked with mud mixed with straw or twigs for a binder. We meant to chink with mortar. But for now those spaces were empty, staring, and wide-eyed.

It never did bother me that people came from everywhere, sidewalk superintendents who looked, shook their heads, and went away laughing. I saw what they saw and I knew how it looked to them, but I also saw a finished house and I knew it would be what architects call a "good" house, a personal house and a home, and gaunt and skeletal as it now was, I loved it.

The fall rains were coming on, now, and we were hurrying to get the roof on. Under a roof much inside work could continue through the winter. Without it, everything would have to come to a halt. Mister G.'s father had finished riving out the ten thousand shingleboards and they had been trucked down to the house where they were stacked in a shed. Now came more advice. "You have to put a board roof on in the dark of the moon."

I grew up with a father who knew moon-science and to some extent practiced it in his gardening, so I had a background for understanding it when Mister G. brought me to Adair County. In planting, things which mature above the ground, such as beans, corn, squash, tomatoes, and so on, are planted in the light of the moon. Things which mature under the ground, such as carrots, potatoes, beets, onions, and so on, must be planted in the dark of the moon. But moon-science is extended into other areas. A split-rail fence must be laid in the light of the moon or the ground rail will sink. A board roof must be put on in the dark of the moon or the ends will curl and it will leak.

I wondered aloud about it. Our neighbor, Ancil Spires, said, "Built me a barn once. Put the boards on one side the roof on in the dark, then I got fidgety and wouldn't wait. Went ahead and put 'em on the other side in the light. Ever' last one of 'em curled up on me and commenced leakin' right straight. Wore out eight years 'fore the others, too."

Not exactly believing but afraid not to believe, we looked at the almanac. The light of the moon is, of course, the waxing moon, from new to full. The dark is the waning moon. "The moon will full next week," Mister G. said.

A week couldn't possibly matter so we decided to wait. Mister G. warned Edgar and Joe to have a full crew ready to begin laying boards at dawn the day following the full moon.

Rain wakened us that morning and it rained buckets all day. It was no little drizzle, either, that country men ignore and work on in. It was a hard heavy rain that would have soaked them to the skin in fifteen minutes. Reporting to work as promised, the men took shelter in the shed and waited for perhaps an hour. No use. It was plain there was going to be no slacking off, so they all went home.

It rained every day for a week, which meant there was only one week left of the dark moon.

There came finally a sunny day and Edgar sent out the call again. The crew responded and worked fast and hard for three days. Then rain again and more rain until the new moon arose. Roofing must end for two weeks.

Rarely have we felt so frustrated. As if to thumb its nose at us the entire two weeks of the light moon was fine. It didn't rain one single day. And we sat twiddling our thumbs and letting it pass. By the time the dark came around again all of us felt poised on the mark, ready for the gun to sound, ready to dash off. The moon fulled and the next morning dawned bright and clear.

This time there were only two days of good weather before the rains came again and again there was no letup until the dark moon was past. Six weeks had now elapsed and the men had worked a total of five days. They had roofed one half of one end of the house. And winter was just around the corner.

To add to our troubles the state of Kentucky, which had

successfully and relentlessly ignored this end of Adair County for a hundred and seventy-five years, decided now was the time to build a new road over the old toll pike.

The first thing the construction crew did was to go down the whole length of the pike and rip out all bridges and culverts and drainage tiles, leaving gaping holes to be driven around on makeshift detours. Daily we had trucks loaded with building materials, lumber, flooring, sand, gravel, concrete, window frames, traveling over the road. And daily they got stuck on one or another of those mushy detours.

Then the construction men began to unload tons of soft, fresh dirt on top of the road to make the roadbed. Ton after ton after ton was dumped. Our trucks had now literally to crawl over and around these massive fills of dirt, and they got stuck even oftener. Our drivers slowly developed a proficiency in profanity that was equal to that of an old-time muleskinner or a top sergeant in the army.

Worst of all, however, was when the drainage tile of our own driveway was unceremoniously yanked out, without so much as a by-your-leave, yet! Within hours a bottomless pit of water and gravel was churned into a morass no truck could cross. Mister G. and Edgar had no alternative except to stop everything and take a full week to hack out a new driveway through the fringe of woods and haul creek gravel to give it some semblance of body.

We felt pretty bitter about that time and wondered if we couldn't sue somebody, especially after Mister G. cracked the oil pan of his big, heavy, low-slung Buick and dragged off three mufflers in a row!

We knew, or *thought* we knew, the new highway would be a rich blessing to the community and we had all hoped it might be built eventually. All of us in the valley, however, began to wonder if the construction engineers knew what they were doing when the fills slowly rose to sky heights and the road took on the look of an earth dam or dike. This is low country admittedly and it was understandable they wanted the road high enough never to be flooded. But did they realize what a dike smack across the middle of the valley would do if Green River ever went on a rampage?

When the new driveway was completed and cars and trucks could crawl inchingly over it, I lost my patience with moon-science. We were having a few sunny days during the light of the moon and I wanted to take advantage of it. "I don't believe in it anyhow," I told Mister G. "Why don't you tell Edgar and Joe to get the crew together and go ahead."

He looked a little doubtful but agreed that at the rate we were going it might easily be spring before the roof was on. Edgar looked even more doubtful and Mister Ancil was just downright mournful. He shook his head ominously. "You'll see," he predicted.

In three sunny days the roofing crew added several laps and then the rains descended again. For a solid week it rained every day and on the final day there was literally a cloud-burst, a white sheet of rain for two hours. We huddled it out in the shed, watching Spout Springs Branch rise slowly to the top of its banks then, awesomely, before our very eyes, inch over. Suddenly Mister G. yelled at me, "Get in the car, quick!"

And just in time, too.

He drove us to high ground and nosed the car against an outbuilding and a little dazed we watched a wall of water rush down the creek, spread ragingly in every direction, and wash the piles of unused logs, the stacks of lumber George had piled up so neatly, the metal roofing from the cottage, the tools, and whatever, downstream before it.

Frightened and awed, I watched the water swirl all around the house, lap at the foundations, and rise along its length. This is it, I thought. If the water reaches the subflooring there's no point finishing this house. Who wants to live with a creek in the living room every year!

But it didn't. It lacked a good foot of reaching the flooring, though it washed all around and under the house. And everybody said so much rain only occurred once every twenty years, and George's mother and father assured us that only once in all their lives had the creek ever got high enough to be a real threat. I had been willing to take a chance on once every twenty years. Now, I wondered. But it certainly *had* been an exceptionally wet autumn and in my own Kentucky years I had never known it to rain so much and so often.

Mister G. sighed with relief when the creek subsided, as quickly as it had risen. "Well, that's been the test," he said. "That's about as high as that creek will ever get. We won't ever have to worry about water in the house."

At midnight last night we were both doing plenty of worrying!

It is February of 1962 as I write. For a week the rains have been falling, a heavy fall occasionally but chiefly the slow, dreary, unremitting drizzle which is so typical of the winter rains in Kentucky. We *can* go, and often do, for as long as four weeks without seeing the sun.

We had a meeting to attend in town last night. Temporarily there was no rain. Both of us glanced at the creek — it is second nature with us when there are these prolonged rains — as we drove away and commented on how little it had risen in spite of the rain.

The meeting was a dinner meeting and all outside sounds were muffled and modified so that none of us knew the rain had begun again until we came out, at ten o'clock, to go home. It was a fairly heavy fall and as we drove the fourteen miles home it became heavier and heavier until finally Mister G. had to pull over to the side of the road and wait for fully thirty minutes while the heavens opened up and dumped tons of water on us. Another cloudburst. We were certain the creek would be out of its banks and wondered if the driveway would be flooded so that we couldn't reach the house.

It was with considerable relief we found the creek in much the same condition as when we left. "Must not have rained so hard here," we said, congratulating ourselves.

We undressed, made ourselves comfortable with cups of hot cocoa and turned on television for the last weather forecast and news.

I don't know what made Mister G. wander out onto the back porch for a last look around before going to bed, but he did. When he came in he quietly began dressing again and advised me to dress also. "Why?"

"The creek is up in the yard," he said.

"Are we going to leave?" I asked, scurrying about for clothing.

He shook his head. "It's too late. We can't drive out and it's much too dangerous to try to wade out in the dark. The current is too swift."

I had to see, of course, and wished instantly I hadn't. It looked to me as if the creek had suddenly shifted its channel and was rushing and gushing and rampaging straight through the yard. Mister G. had turned on a spotlight upstairs and directed it into the back yard, which no longer remotely resembled the back yard. It looked like the surf at Miami Beach during an Atlantic storm. There were even white-capped waves as the raging water rushed around trees and fence posts and shrubs and the car. As I watched, with cold fear settling in my stomach, a whole tree came floating down, turning slowly and swirling, caught here and then there by the current. Fascinated and almost hypnotized by its movement I thought it would be borne straight into the house. At the last moment some whim of the current took it away, turned it over and sent it on down the main channel.

Only a few times in my life have I known what it is to be totally helpless. This was one of them. We were wholly helpless to help ourselves. High land was only three hundred yards away but between us and high land was a raging flood of water through which, in the dark, it would have been suicidal to try to wade. The car motor would have drowned out instantly had we tried to drive out, to say nothing of such an attempt being extremely hazardous with no road showing, maybe no road there, and all landmarks distorted.

I glanced at the clock and saw it was only eleven-thirty. I wandered through the house wondering where to begin first to stack rugs and mattresses and loose objects off the floor, and where to stack them, and whether we shouldn't begin moving as much as we could upstairs. But there was such a lot of everything. Before we could get half through, I thought, the creek would be all over the house.

I peered through the windows toward the highway and saw that we were alone in our vigil. Not a light was showing from our neighbors' homes. I determined, then, where our action had to lie. I would take water, the coffee maker, food, cigarettes, a change of clothing, upstairs so that we could retreat there when the time came and be reasonably comfortable until morning. Somebody, I knew, would rescue us with a boat once daylight had come. And the flood waters could have their way downstairs.

When I had done all I could do I made a fresh pot of coffee and sat down to wait. Under the floor I could hear the flood gurgling and roaring and knew that if I could see outside at that moment I would see nothing but that rampaging creek on all sides. It was a moment of truth, I can assure you. I wondered why I had ever thought I loved water!

Mister G., in his fishing waders, was paddling around outside adding to my fears. Who could tell what potholes were being formed into which he might step. Or the current might sweep him off his feet. Or he might, in the distortion of night and water, mistake his footing. Or a log or another tree might rush down on him and bear him away. But he refused to heed my pleas to come inside. He was too restless and excited.

The utility room which contains the electric pump as well as the other contrivances all utility rooms hold was one step down, six inches, below the kitchen. I had determined that when water crept in there it would be time to move the things I had packed upstairs and to *make* Mister G. come in and go upstairs with me.

It came.

Slowly, now, the water inched under the door and spread in a widening shallow circle — not the gush I had envisioned. I yelped for Mister G. and he came to the outside door, peered in and shook his head. "That's as high as it will get," he said, "don't worry."

I stood guard over the utility room and to my amazement

he was right. The circle of water never rose over the entire floor and within ten minutes it began to subside and ten minutes later there was just a wet stain to show it had ever been inside at all.

Then Mister G. came in and asked for a cup of coffee. He was grinning. "It's going down now. Falling. The worst is over."

I looked at the clock again. Midnight. In an hour and a half the creek had risen swiftly, crested, and begun to fall. I felt weak and trembly and a little sick at my stomach. Mister G. made me a big, stiff hot toddy and held it under my nose. "Drink this and go to bed. Sleep, now. Everything's all right."

But it was two-thirty before I slept and Mister G. didn't take his clothes off all night. Around two I glanced up toward the highway again and this time every house was blazing with lights and there was a considerable amount of traffic going up and down the road. "What's happening?" I asked.

"The river," Mister G. said. "The water is probably rising on the other side of the road."

Two cars, one at each of our driveways, were parked with their lights turned in the direction of our house. From the reflection of their lights we could see that a huge lake lay between us and the highway. But it caused me no troublesome thoughts now. The creek was draining off and Spout Springs House was safe.

Our crisis passed at midnight. But the farmers of the valley faced theirs now as the river, fed by multiple creeks like our Spout Springs, poured their tons of water down these long steep watersheds into its maw.

I awakened shortly after daybreak this morning. We were

dry and the creek was flowing as mildly and sweetly as it
ever does, well within its banks. But it looks odd and
strangely different. Tons of gravel have been washed down
and cut new channels and turns and made new gravel bars.
Our long driveway, the principal one, is ruined. Swiftly
washed gravel has scoured and gutted it into little more than
a ditch and left strange heaps and mounds of sand and gravel
in new places. Logs and drift and trash are heaped all over
our meadow and the yard is a chaos of drift and sand and
gravel. But at its worst Spout Springs Branch only came
knocking at our door. Mister G. had shrewdly built the
house high enough that its flooring stands higher than
the road. Never, he tells me, will Spout Springs Branch flow
through our house. "Why," I wail, "didn't you tell me that
last night?"

"I thought you knew," he answers mildly.

It seems I'll never quit learning how this house got built!

Green River, this morning, is rampaging and families who
never before have been threatened are being evacuated by
boat. The highway is doing its damage. Where before
when Green River went spreading over the bottoms, it spread
gently and not too deeply, the highway balks it now, makes
a dike, and everyone living between the road and the river
has water from six inches to two feet in homes never touched
by the river before. Old-timers are shaking their heads this
morning and saying there has never been such a disastrous
flood in this valley. Why, I wonder, if they were going to
make a levee of the highway, didn't they build it along the
river, make it reinforce the riverbank? Why build a levee
straight down the middle of the valley?

They followed the old toll pike, of course. But the old

toll pike lay level with fields and meadows. When, occasionally, there was a flood the water spread over the road and for a day or two traffic was halted. This, naturally, was an inconvenience but it was nothing compared to what our people are enduring today. The water could spread out, shallowly, and back up each little ravine and hollow. It threatened no lives and damaged few, if any, homes. Nobody had to be evacuated. Everyone knew, from experience, how high the flood waters would reach and nobody worried. Some stock might have to be brought out of the bottoms, but nobody's home would be invaded.

This flood, with two new highways crisscrossing the valley, has been a new experience. The water, held and balked by the road dikes, has had no place to go but up, and our valley people have suffered untold damage and destruction. So much for progress! Like my youngest grandson, who mourned when the highway by our house was being built that it was ruining all the prettiest places, I'm ag'in it. So much that is counted as progress is not progress at all. So much of it is intermingled with the expediency of politics. A campaign promise to build a road is made, and eventually the promise is kept, cheaply and without foresight. I've heard a local politician say, laughingly, that a road promised is better than a road built. This morning I couldn't agree more heartily and I wish our road was still only a promise.

When that first swift spreading of Spout Springs Branch had just as swiftly subsided the sun came out for a few days. To our horror then we noticed the last three laps of shingleboards turning up their toes. "What's the matter with them?" I asked Edgar.

Edgar grinned. "That's the three laps we put on in the light of the moon."

Mister G. surveyed them morosely. "You'll have to rip 'em off, Edgar."

Edgar nodded. "Figured we would when we put 'em down."

Mr. Ancil Spires sauntered over to say I told you so, but he said it mildly and even gently. "Just don't do to go ag'in the signs," he said. "I knowed this would happen."

I meant to get at the bottom of this. "Why," I asked, "what difference can the moon make?"

Mister Ancil, who whittles constantly, picked up a twig and unjacked his knife, slid a few curls from the twig and said, quietly, "Well, the moon draws mighty powerful when it's moving towards the full. Way I've got it figgered, it just draws them shingleboards into curls is all."

It was as good an explanation as any. And, I thought wearily, if the moon causes the tides there is no good reason why it shouldn't make shingleboards curl. Who knows what the moon can do? Certainly not I. But I now knew one thing we had to do. Roof only in the dark of the moon. If it took all winter it would just have to take all winter. There was no use battling the pulling power of the moon.

Chapter 11
Welcome to Cathay

OLD-TIMERS in Kentucky have a lot of weather sayings that are right a little better than fifty percent of the time, which at least gives them an edge over a wild guess. These old sayings have been handed down from generation to generation and were originally based on the close observation of men who had no recourse to weather bureaus or prophets. Each man was a prophet himself.

I don't recall that I ever thought about weather when I lived in the city. I might be uncomfortably warm or uncomfortably cold or uncomfortably wet, but it never occurred to me to study the sky or the wind or the clouds, and a barometer was something I had only read about. I had certainly never heard of any tried and trusted weather portents such as all country people know. I might take a quick look out the window as I dressed for the office to see whether I needed an umbrella but that was all.

Almost the first thing you learn when you move to the country, however, is that weather is all-important and very shortly you begin to watch cloud formations, notice wind changes, and take note of all natural phenomena. Nowadays when I am awakened on a February night by the flash of lightning and the roll of thunder automatically I say to myself, "Thunder in February, frost in May." It works out that way more than half the time.

Mister G. and I compete with each other to see who will be first to hear a katydid in the summer. We begin listening, with considerable concentration, around the fifth of July for though they vary as much as three weeks you will rarely hear one earlier than that. When the familiar rasp is finally heard we mark it on the big kitchen calendar, saying, "Ninety days to frost."

On the morning of the first big general frost in October we look back to our marked date in July. It's amazing how often the katydid has hit it right on the nose, or missed only by a day or two. I don't know the answer. I can only surmise that katydids have a built-in thermostat, some instinct for their own life-span, for precisely the ninety days he can rasp out his eternal indecision as to whether katy did or katy didn't.

It's safe to plant corn when the first whippoorwill is heard. There will be no more frost. And a child may take off his long underwear and shuck his shoes and stockings to go barefoot when the first butterfly is sighted. The back of winter is broken and he'll not take cold.

When cows huddle close together in the pasture and turn

their rumps to the north, no matter how mild the day is, get ready for a weather change. It's going to snow or freeze or blow a norther. The same is true when pigs squeal. Weather is breeding.

You can tell how long a summer rain is going to last by watching the chickens. If they take shelter, the rain will last quite a spell. If they continue to pick and feed, it'll be over soon.

There is one saying which I have never, not even once, known to be wrong. "When the chimney smokes, weather's breeding." Any day the smoke churns down the flue of our fireplace instead of drawing straight up as it usually does so beautifully, I don't even bother to look at the barometer. I know it's falling and I know that no matter how blue the sky is a storm is brooding and will be lashing at us within twenty-four hours. I have never seen that sign fail. I recall a morning when I looked out the bedroom window to see a beautiful day, not a cloud in the sky, but the neighbor's smokes were all dashing downward. As balmy as it was, as warm and bright, before nightfall a blizzard was sending snow in raging flurries down our valley. That sign bats a thousand percent.

But the weather saying which affected us most the winter we were building the house was, "There'll be as many snows as the day of the month of the first fall."

We had the first light skift of snow that year on the twenty-eighth of October. In vexing frustration I counted the snows as they came and melted and came again and the saying outdid itself. Instead of twenty-eight, we had thirty-two and that doesn't often happen in Kentucky.

Our house sat and sat with its poor hat off and its walls and subflooring soaking up the rains and snows, the north wind blowing through its cracks and ice glazing the logs. All work had to stop. It was perishing cold and no man, except the abominable snowman, could have worked with icicles dripping from his nose, with frozen nails burning his fingers, with hammers that split their handles with a loud crack, and with teeth playing a drum roll on each other as they tried to clench together. Nothing to do, we said, but wait.

Normally Mister G. and I can settle into November and December and January and February quite cozily. For the unfriendly outdoors there is the friendly compensation of a fire, drawn curtains, endless pots of coffee, dozens of books to be read and, for me, the best time of the year to work. It is so naturally a time of hibernation that I can sink into the writing of a book, withdraw from time and man, and do it more easily than at any other time of the year. There is a long silence and a long peace and if I'm lucky enough to keep both unbroken I can do prodigious amounts of good work.

But this was a different winter and the house should have been moving along. It couldn't, so, exasperated, I wrote and wrote and wrote on the book which was eventually called *The Land Beyond the Mountains.* But even as I wrote I dreamed of spring and of how our house would look in the spring. And I made notes of trees and shrubs to be brought down from the hills. "More trees?" Mister G. sighed.

But I wanted something of the natural disorder of the woods, so I jotted down wild plum, dogwood, redbud, swamp maple, a pine or two, some papaws and a sarvisberry and a few willows. We lost the dogwood, the swamp maple and the wild plum, but we proudly point to a redbud, one pine, one papaw, one sarvisberry and one willow that lived and throve.

I wanted lots of flowering weeds and herbs, spiderwort, Queen Anne's lace, costmary, henbane, marjoram, and more than anything I wanted a shrub of rosemary. This is the shrub that will never grow taller than Christ was tall and will never grow another inch after thirty-three years. I have never got my rosemary tree, nor have I ever got the Christmas roses at the door to ward off evil. I have had to rely upon making a cross in the ashes of the fire each night to keep wailing and restless spirits from wandering. But I needn't have worried about spiderwort and Queen Anne's lace. Both grow about like jungle webs and are likely some day to take over the place.

I wanted the house to look so old no one could imagine its having a beginning — to look as if, with some sort of divine leavening in the soil, it had grown where it was, chimney rocks, logs, shingleboards and all. And because it sits a little way off the road perhaps there was some hope it might be a little hard to find. No hope was ever more forlorn.

When I began writing I was not prepared for the reader's consuming interest in a writer's personal life, his home, his appearance and his conversation, his hopes and aspirations. In my ignorance I had supposed that nothing could be more private than a writer's solitary communion with his muse. The possibility of the daily mail being freighted with letters from readers, or the front door being opened to total strangers whose only introduction is always, "I have read your books," never occurred to me.

Through stories about us and the way we lived down here in the hills, people began to find the road to us. In the beginning it found me stiff and embarrassed, but as the years have passed and more and more people have written and more and more people have come, I have grown accustomed to it and have learned to think of it as a tribute. Not so my family to whom I am not a writer but a daughter, a mother, a grandmother, a sister. They are appalled and I am occasionally hard put to it to keep them from insulting "invaders." We have some hilarious contretemps when any of them are visiting during the "tourist season."

With few exceptions the people who come are friendly and warmly generous, and many have become good friends. The exceptions have provided some salt for the diet. They are the curious who ask point-blank questions about your personal and private life, who collect souvenirs even if they have to steal them, who treat your home as if it were a public museum.

Two carloads, packed to the windows, drove up one Sunday afternoon. They piled out, turned the children loose to romp in the yard, and invaded the house. I use the word advisedly. Without so much as a by-your-leave the women sauntered through every room fingering the curtain materials, poking the upholstering of chairs and sofas, rummaging bookshelves and magazine racks, ruffling bedspreads, handling pictures and leaving them askew. Short of ordering them out of the house I didn't know what to do except follow them around sort of helplessly trying to keep them from doing any more damage than possible. But in spite of me they managed to sneak out three cloisonné ashtrays as souvenirs.

Mister G. was meantime trying to corral the little demons masquerading as children who had chased a calf until it was ready to drop, had broken a limb off an apple tree, and had scared the hens into such a trauma they didn't lay an egg for ten days.

This kind of thing happens just often enough that if strangers aren't willing to come in and sit down quietly when they enter, Mister G. gets a signal to stick around. Four eyes are better than two and we have lost too many small and sometimes precious objects not to view rovers with some doubt. I still grieve over a bisque figurine which belonged to my grandmother and a small crayon drawing my first grandson did when he was four years old. Loose manuscript pages have a way of disappearing, too, from my desk.

Another kind of caller, since we have no telephones in our part of the county, is the pleader for a cause or a drive or a crusade or a municipal or civic project. These are always worthy causes and on the surface it looks extremely selfish of us not to lend ourselves to them. One of the most difficult things to explain is that a writer's commitment is total and unending and that his books must be his "good works." There is simply not time for more.

It sounds so arrogant, however, to say so. But to interrupt a work week for committee or board meetings, for planning sessions, is not quite the same for a writer as it is for even the busiest business man or woman. I know because I have been a business woman and am now a writer. The two are not remotely the same. With a writer an interruption causes a hiatus in the rhythm of work, in broken concentration, which cannot easily be picked up or quickly abridged. A meeting which lasts only one hour, to which a business man or woman can come, give his attention, then return to his own affairs, can cause a distraction of concentration with a writer it may take two days to mend. A talk or speech of even the most informal kind, when a book is in progress, may disrupt for as long as two weeks. I despair of having this understood however and have resigned myself to being thought coldly selfish and uninterested. It is one of the prices that must be paid for that yearly book.

Twice, and I am lucky it hasn't happened oftener, persons have come with no purpose except to quarrel with me. No writer can hope to satisfy every reader and I have sense enough to know that what I write doesn't please everybody. I don't intend it to. I please myself as well as I am able and the chips can fall where they will. I can get tremblingly angry with people who come into my home, without invitation, only to be rude to me, but I usually contain my anger and point out merely that nobody is required to read me. They have only to refuse to read another word of mine and they'll be rid of me, but that doesn't seem to be the point. In both cases the persons were filled with self-importance that could only be satisfied by confronting me personally to point out how wrong or unjust I had been.

My reader mail has been blessedly free of crackpot letters, also. In conversation with other writers I have learned how little of this crank kind of mail I have had to endure. But I do recall vividly a series of homemade postcards that arrived, one each week for four weeks, from southern California. They were anonymous, naturally. Each postcard was outsize, cut apparently from shirtboards. My picture, clipped from book jackets, was pasted on the address side above my name, also cut from book jackets, and the reverse side of the card was liberally filled with quotations from the Bible in red and blue crayon. None of them were inimical or hate-filled, but none of them made the least bit of sense either. Knowing that southern California harbors some queer religious sects we finally concluded that somebody was proselytizing in a most unique way. But what he was proselytizing we couldn't make out. At any rate the cards stopped coming as abruptly as they had begun. The sender must have given up on me. Since he had never signed his name it puzzled us what he could have expected. Mister G. thought he may have inhabited a mental institution.

One of my early books was *Tara's Healing* which described, with much sympathy, a religious sect which have maintained a missionary work in Adair County for many years. They are known locally as the White Caps because of the pretty little white caps the women wear at all times. Their denominational name, however, is the Church of the Brethren in Christ. I have been told that former President Eisenhower's mother was a member of this church but I have never tried to verify it.

When this book came out there was a considerable amount of mail expressing interest in the theology of the denomination. I had had the generous cooperation of the church itself in writing the book and the superintendent for Kentucky, Mr. Elam O. Dohner, kindly allowed me to give him the letters for reply. I felt inadequate to deal with theological questions. I doubt there were any converts to the denomination but it was interesting to see how many people had lost their early faith and were groping for something to take its place.

After *40 Acres and No Mule* was published I had a long and sorrowful letter from a woman in Colorado who was a vegetarian. She moaned at length because Mister G. and I ate fish and turtle soup and fried squirrel and other meats. I particularly recall that she took offense at my statement that Mister G. gave a fish a sporting chance. She said the fish was hurt just as badly when he was caught by a sportsman as when he was caught in a fish trap. There is no answer to that kind of letter and I don't try to give one. They go into the wastebasket.

Once a Theosophist, southern California again, wrote quite fully, reams in fact, about his philosophy, all of it way over my head, proposing that I join his group in their search for Truth. I skimmed through trying to find the point and found it in his final paragraph. He wanted a donation.

There are many requests for donations — donations of money for almost every cause under the sun, for clothing, for recipes I personally use — churchwomen making up cookbooks — for money, for the use of my name on letterheads, and always and forever for free books. It would be impossible to guess at how often an author is asked to give his books and the requests range from a bold effort to obtain the full set of his works to a timid appeal for one. It is also impossible to give all the books one is asked to give. Every time there is such a request I try to appraise the request and make a decision accordingly. Shut-ins, people who write from a rest home or hospital or nursing home, invariably get a book, for I have never known them to ask for more than one. Certain hospitals are on the permanent mailing list with my publisher. And I am glad to give at least one copy of each new book to certain small and struggling libraries. One request infuriates me. Certain little poetry clubs or essay clubs or insignificant little short story clubs are forever having book fairs. They furnish their stalls with free copies from the authors they can inveigle. I fell for this for a year or two but it has been a long time since I sent a free copy for anybody's Book Fair. Let them buy them.

Perhaps the letter which caused us the most alarm and called for the swiftest and most decisive action was one from an obvious tramp in New Jersey. He proposed that he come at once and live with us! He said he had always wanted to live on a farm and while he had had no experience in farm work he was in the prime of life, he was healthy and he was strong. It took some doing to persuade him we could not give him a home and for several months I felt considerable apprehension every time a stranger appeared at the door. I was afraid he might have taken to the road before our lawyer's letter reached him and would turn up on our doorstep. I didn't feel entirely safe for a good three months.

Some great treasures have dropped into our laps, however, through the mail and at our door, chiefly through the latter. There comes knocking often a person we would not willingly have missed knowing. Such were the nice middle-aged couple who drove from western Kansas just to spend one day on our ridge. They lived on a big wheat farm near the Colorado line and they had never before been east of the Mississippi River. They knew no one in Kentucky. But it was the slack season of the year and having just read *40 Acres and No Mule* they decided to see our forty acres and ourselves.

They arrived in Columbia, our county seat town, on a Saturday and they stayed overnight in a motel there. The next morning they set out and stopped at the crossroads store to provision themselves with a picnic lunch and to ask directions to our place. They had no intention, they said, of bothering us but would we mind, did anybody think, if they just drove past and took some pictures of our house?

They were told we wouldn't mind. "They're as common as an old shoe," they were told, "and if you'll just go up and knock they'll make you welcome." Bless our neighbors. They are so pestered so often. They must grow very weary of giving directions, but they never let it show. The first evidence of good manners the stranger in our parts has is not from us, but from the people who must direct the stranger to our door.

Encouraged, this middle-aged couple did then drive into our driveway and stop. We found them completely endearing and it was our pleasure to give them a big Sunday dinner and to show them a Kentucky hill farm. They shook their heads over the farm, not understanding how a living could be made from such rocks and hills and hollows. We assured them it was a very poor living, not at all to be compared with that of their big wheat farm. We still exchange Christmas cards with them and we do mean, sometime, when driving west to stop by their farm in western Kansas.

There is a man in Missouri who brought several boys from an orphanage to see us. We loved that day. With great courtesy the boys rambled over the farm, drew water from the well, played gently with the dogs, watched the cows in the pasture and rode the horse. Reminded of their manners when it was time to leave they said thank you sweetly and waved to us until they were out of sight down the road. I have always been glad they came and had such an exciting and wonderful day on our farm.

There was a young nun once who took so literally the characters in one of the books that she could not believe they were fictional. She came from Pennsylvania hoping to see the place where they lived, expecting to renew her acquaintance with them by touching the walls of their homes and by walking where they had walked. She was quietly disappointed to learn they were all people of my imagination but she recovered and before she left asked if she might have a flower from my nondescript flower bed. I am grateful for the memory of her gentle warmth.

Kentucky teachers bring their English classes to visit and Kentucky college students writing a term paper on one of the books or their author come for interviews. Readers who are driving through the state make detours to visit an hour or two, and out-of-state visitors to relatives in the area like to come. For a few years we kept a guest book but when we had logged guests from every state in the union we abandoned it. It seemed part and parcel of the law of diminishing returns.

My mother was spending a summer with us one year when we still had the big farm. A car with a California license drove up and out of it crawled a plumpish old gentleman of about seventy. I think I was cleaning a chicken but whatever I was doing I was caught in the back yard and dropping my task I went to meet him. His old face beamed and he shouted at me, "You are Janice Holt Giles!"

I admitted I was.

He broke into a trot and before I knew what was happening he enveloped me in a rib-breaking hug. He must, I thought frantically, be some long-lost relative and I looked at my mother over his shoulder hoping she would recognize him. If this was Great-uncle Charlie from Fresno I wanted to know it. She shook her head.

I extricated myself from his arms eventually and stood apart while he eyed me mistily and happily. "I am Dr. Blank," he announced, "from Carmel-by-the-sea. I have driven four thousand miles to see you!"

As weak as my arithmetic is I knew it wasn't four thousand miles from the Pacific to central Kentucky, but I let it stand. If he wanted four thousand miles let him have four thousand miles. I led him into the house. Before the morning was over I wished I hadn't. I wished Carmel-by-the-sea had kept him. He was the most active old grasshopper I ever hope to see! He had either a finger or his nose into everything all morning long. We were actively farming that year and work couldn't stop for him.

My mother was churning when he drove up and when she saw that he meant to stay a spell she went back to it. He went with her and he looked on and when she took up the butter he dabbled a dirty finger in it to taste it. "Haven't tasted country butter in forty years," he caroled, "my, that's good!" Mother promptly gave him the whole batch. We wouldn't have touched it after he'd stuck his finger in it.

Then he had to sample the well water. "Never was better water than in these country wells," he said.

He had to feed the chickens, though they didn't need it, and he had to wander out to the pasture and look over the cows. Then he had to follow Mister G. to the field and ride, perilously, the back bar of the tractor. I held my breath until he had made a safe round and was back on dry land again. "Plowed with mules in my time," he said, "better get you a good team of mules, boy, if you want to farm right."

I had desperately resigned myself to his staying for lunch but to my great relief he left as suddenly and as explosively

as he had come. He nearly drove off into the hollow as he
went down the road, peering back at us and waving. "God!"
Mister G. said, dropping to a lawn chair.

My mother sniffed and said, "Why do you put up with
that kind of boor?"

I poked the chicken liver inside the back to keep it from
spattering and refrained from answering. You put up with
it because everybody who buys a book feels as if he owns
a little piece of you. And maybe he does. You can argue
all day long that you and your typewriter turn out your
books and earn your living. When the chips are down it's
the people who buy them who feed you and clothe you and
put money in your bank account. You can argue all day
long that the public has all they're entitled to when they've
read what you've written and you are entitled to your pri-
vacy. They don't think so. At least they don't think so
about me. One of my trademarks is the warm and friendly
feeling my readers have toward me. When they come to my
home they don't feel as if they're coming to the home of a
stranger. They feel as if they're coming to the home of a
good friend. Hundreds of them have every book I've written and wait eagerly for the next one. They get me all
mixed up with the characters I've created and they know
that the person who dreamed up Miss Willie and Hannah
Fowler and Johnny Osage and Savanna will understand immediately how much they love those people and her, and they
never doubt their welcome, and so help me they *will* be
welcome. Some of them are boors but most of them are
wonderful, warm, generous, admiring, friendly followers. I
owe them a tremendous debt and I mean to pay it.

One kind of caller, however, I do wish would pass me

by. That's the stranger who, after half an hour of general conversation, suddenly plumps a manuscript into my lap and says, breathlessly, "I have written a book, too. And I *know*, I just know it's a good book. But nobody will publish it. It's the story of my life and all my friends say I've had a most unusual life and they have all urged me to write a book about it."

Sometimes it's the story of a grandfather who was a Confederate general, or a parent who homesteaded land in Texas, or an uncle who went to the Klondike, or an aunt who was a missionary in China. "I just know if you would read it and tell me . . . if you would take it and rewrite it . . . if you would help me get it published . . . I'd be willing to pay you . . . you could have half the profits, but I'd want my name to be featured . . ."

Every last one of these stories is good, I have no doubt. Any professional writer could take them and make them into a book. But why should he? For my own part, I won't live long enough to write the books I have in mind. I got started late. And for anybody interested, I didn't have any help. I wrote my books, I sent them to a publisher, raw and cold and stark. They stood on their own two feet, just as my mother had taught me. I didn't ask anybody to help me. I just sat down in front of a typewriter and wrote books. Then I sent them to publishers. It happens that the very first book I wrote was accepted by a publisher. But nobody interceded for me. And I deny furiously that it was luck. No publisher is going to take a book unless he thinks it will sell. I had stuffed myself with books from the time I was four years old. Like a sponge I had absorbed the technique of writing. When I finally sat down in front of a typewriter to write a book of my own, the technique came easily and naturally to me. I had read, for thirty years, an average of one book a day. I have little patience with people who have read perhaps fewer than a hundred books in a lifetime but because they have lived want to write a book about it.

It is always a sad moment when these situations arise for if I don't read the manuscript, or cooperate, I have made an enemy and if I *do* read it, and there is usually no merit and I must say so, I have also made an enemy. I could never take another person's story and write it so that solution is automatically out, and I have learned over the years that few people asking for criticism really want it. What they want to hear is praise, the beautiful words that they have written a masterpiece and that I will promptly see to it that my publisher takes it, and that in no time at all they, too, will have the thrilling experience of seeing their names on the spine of a book and will be rolling in royalty checks.

Two people only who have come to me for critical advice have taken it well and tried valiantly to better their material. The usual reaction is a stiffening and a stubborn defense. "I don't agree with you. I like it the way it is. That's the way I want it published."

To that I can only say, "Fine. Then get it published the way it is."

A conviction has grown in me that most people who think they want to write don't really. What they want is to be writers — the prestige, perhaps the fame — though it comes to few — without the work.

I have no convictions about whether writers are born or made. Maybe it's a little bit of both. I would guess you must be born articulate and imaginative, then learn the techniques of the trade. But I do have some strong convictions about what makes a durable professional writer. First, he wants to write more than he wants to do anything else in the world. He wants to write more than he wants to party and play, travel, earn more money more easily, gain prestige and power in any other field. I don't know why anybody should, but the genuine article, the real producing writer, does.

Next he is persistent. He is almost totally undiscourageable. Rebuffed by one editor he plods on to another. He doesn't give up easily. In fact he doesn't give up at all. He's in there fighting all the time. If he did give up, he'd never get published.

Third, he is capable of very hard work and very lonely work for very long periods of time. When he sits down to begin a book he voluntarily makes a jailbird out of himself for a year, two years, maybe three. He does it knowing that he has turned the key himself. Nobody asks him to write that book, but he has to and he knows the only way to do it is to go to his desk every morning, every week, every month until he has come to the end. All producing and selling writers have this quality of self-discipline, for nobody is boss and nobody sets a time clock for them and nobody really cares whether they write or not.

I have no golden key of entry either to my agent or to my publisher. Nobody has. If I asked either of them to read a manuscript I thought had merit they certainly would, for nobody knows how eager all people connected with book publishing are for new talent. But what gets a book published, and no strings can be pulled for it, is merit and nothing else. If you have faithfully sent a manuscript out and keep getting it back, somewhere along the line you had better sit down and take stock. One publisher can be wrong, two can be wrong, or five or six. But when enough have turned your story in its present form down there's no use feeling aggrieved. Better look over the material and get busy with it if you've been lucky enough to get some editorial suggestions. Or junk it and start again. This is where most amateurs quit. They're convinced they have written a good book and they grow angry when it doesn't sell and childishly accuse the entire publishing business of failing to recognize their unique talent. Any time you've got real talent what you write is going to be published.

I have had extremely good fortune in writing and nobody knows it better than I, but both my agent and my publisher will vouch for the fact that there isn't a harder working writer in the business today. Writing is a full-time job with me just as practicing medicine is for a doctor, practicing law for a lawyer, teaching school for a teacher, and just as no principled person would allow his personal preferences to interfere with his work, I don't allow any to interfere with mine. Year in and year out, I'm at it.

Although my work had always required a lot of writing, none of it had been fiction. I had never considered attempting fiction until I began writing it more or less as a sideline, at night after a full day in the dean's office at the Presbyterian Seminary in Louisville. Mister G. and I were struggling along the first winter after our marriage while he went to school on the G.I. bill and it seemed a good idea to earn a little extra money if I could. He certainly couldn't. He was in a schoolroom all day and had his head buried in textbooks until midnight every night. I at least had my evenings free. We toyed around with plot ideas until we came up with a pretty good one which I fooled with and elaborated and eventually began to set down on paper. As the story grew it took hold of us and we set up a regular schedule. When I came home from the office around five-thirty, Mister G. had dinner started and we finished it up together, washed the dishes, then he settled to his studies in one corner of the room while my typewriter clacked away in another corner. I set myself a rigid three hours, no matter how tired or headachy, or uninspired I was, and whether the work went well or not, I plugged away from seven-thirty to ten-thirty.

I have always thought it was a combination of two things which made the book acceptable — it had a picturesque setting, the Kentucky hills, and the story was fairly warm and moving. At that time I loved lots of lyrical adjectives and metaphors and they are strewn thickly over the pages. I'm not sure all that "pretty" writing didn't help sell the book for there are many, many people, as I learned from reader reaction, who like that kind of writing. I got hundreds of letters quoting particular purple patches back at me.

Later I developed a very lean prose style in keeping with the frontier people about whom I wrote in the historical series. In 1775 in Kentucky people didn't go in for purple patches and since I get inside characters so much when I write I could no more use them than the people themselves would have. There are still people, especially Kentuckians, who frankly confess they liked the early books best, but the wide readership came only when I began writing history.

And it is history. A novelist doesn't have to be entirely authentic with his facts. He can take a good deal of leeway, but I never have. I never have felt it necessary. I hit upon a device quite early which weaves a fictional plot with a few fictional characters into an interesting time, among real and genuine historical figures, and I have never had the least difficulty sticking strictly to the facts as far as the events and actual people were concerned. In fact, I find it an invaluable aid to plotting. Some fabulous things have happened on the frontiers of our country and all I have to do is hit upon an especially vivid piece of time and place and build a story into it.

When I first had the idea of doing a frontier series it seemed to me the books would flow better and have more continuity if I created several families to work with and if I intermarried them and shifted them about and let the varying members and generations carry the series forward. That's the way, after all, history really happens. The sons of early Kentuckians moved on to Missouri and Kansas and Oklahoma and their sons moved on to the Spanish territories, the Oregon territory and California.

It was a happy idea. No book is a sequel to any other. Each one can be read for itself and if the reader is not familiar with any of the other books he is not aware of any lack. But if he is a faithful follower he rejoices when one of the old familiar characters turns up again. Running into him, they write me, is like meeting an old friend again. And I am happy working with these people.

In many ways they are more real to me than people of flesh and bones because I know them in ways no living human being can ever truly know another. They have no secrets from me and they never behave in bewildering and confusing ways. Even when they get stubborn and cantankerous I know which headstrong strain is pulling at the bit and I just pull a little harder myself and remind them that's their gutter-snipe grandmother showing up, or that's their wailing, weeping aunt making them afraid of life, or that's the restless wind of a romantic grandfather making them act silly. I know their backgrounds so well, the environment that has shaped them, as well as the family lines, the social conditions they have grown up in, the speech that is natural to them, the thinking common to their time and place, their whole frame of reference.

I don't know what I shall do if I ever come to the end of the series. Feel like death probably. Certainly my world without the Fowlers and Cartwrights and Coopers will be far emptier.

Chapter 12
Shaped-Note Style

" . . . I will do strongly before the sun and moon whatever
inly rejoices me, and the heart appoints."

Mr. Ralph Waldo Emerson may have done strongly before
the sun and moon whatever inly rejoiced him but we couldn't.
The moon was against it. We would have inly rejoiced very
much if the weather had cleared for just two weeks while the
moon was dark so our house could be roofed and this was
what our hearts appointed. Nature, however, paid no heed
to inly rejoicements and heart appointments and skies continued to weep and mourn.

Having now committed ourselves to inactivity until this sodden world should dry out, we turned our backs on the house, refused to look at its tipsy, water-soaked walls any longer, and went with Pansy and Russell Phillips for Thanksgiving with the bachelors in Bowling Green.

Very high among those friends we enjoy is a small group who, through the bonds of individual friendships at first, and a little bit of the hand of fate, have slowly become so congenial as to form a special coterie who foregather often at Spout Springs. There are five men whom we speak of as the "bachelors," Pansy and Russell Phillips and ourselves.

This small coterie had its inception in the original friendship with the first of the bachelors, William Marshall Lowe. We were living in the apartment in Campbellsville and Mister G. was working on the *News-Journal*. A young man full of wit and fun, with an unusual talent for enjoying life and with an excellent baritone voice which broke into song without provocation, dropped into the office daily to exchange quips with one of the girls. Mister G. brought him home with him one day and we have held him to us with hooks of steel ever since.

That same year, on a gray Thanksgiving Day, Buddy (nobody calls him William Marshall) brought Mitchell Leichhardt and Joe Covington to us. Both men live in Bowling Green where Mitchell is a landscape gardener. He is a gentleman, literate, cultivated, traveled, truly civilized. He is guileless, unmalicious, sweet, slow-spoken, loyal, chivalrous and untiresomely cerebral.

We first felt the leading hand of fate when we learned, almost at once, that Mitchell had been in the Air Corps during the war and that on overseas duty he had been stationed with the 15th in Italy at precisely the same time as Libby's husband

and very near the same air base. When he spoke with familiarity of the same towns and the same officers we realized that undoubtedly, on big bombing missions which required an entire wing, the two young men had flown together. They even went on leave to the same places and we wonder if they might not have met, missed the significance of names — and there was no good reason then why they shouldn't — and forgotten. For his own sake we would love him, but it has at least added a spice of interest to speculate on the missions and other places Mitch and Nash may have been together.

Joe Covington is the city attorney of Bowling Green and rarely have we known a more sparkling, witty, scintillating individual. He is also honorable, responsible, and life has already tempered him into fine metal. It was not revealed to us immediately how his own experiences were entangled with those of my daughter. We simply enjoyed him and felt any "getherin'" of the clan without him was dull and lusterless.

The following summer, 1956, Buddy Lowe led us to Pansy and Russell Phillips. I had heard much of them from him already. They lived in Greensburg, as did Buddy, and they had known him all his life. From him I knew that Pansy was a painter and indeed I even had one of her oils he had given me. I knew she was the guiding spirit behind the Greensburg Art Club, a group of women who had a studio where they could paint as they pleased and to which Pansy devoted a good bit of her spare time.

Buddy asked me one day if I would like to go with him to their summer show. I was pleased to go.

And I was more than pleased with Pansy Phillips. I have not forgotten my first impression of her, a woman as tall and as rawboned as I, whose eyes looked levelly into mine and whose mouth, wide and generous, grinned warmly at me. I noted the strong structure of her face, the slightly crooked teeth, the slightly grayed hair, and heard her rich, loamy voice making me welcome. I am not an infallible judge of people. Nobody is. But Pansy Phillips excited me and I sensed that here was a woman who, understanding the requirements of friendship well, would, if she gave you her friendship, be like the Rock of Gibraltar in your life forevermore. And it has so proved.

Even when I was a child friendships that put chains on me, that tried to possess me, irked me. Pansy is the least demanding friend I have ever had. There isn't an ounce of possessiveness in her. She hasn't time for it. Her own life is too full, and more than anyone else outside the family she understands and respects the demands writing makes upon one.

She is pretty frank and outspoken, even, if she weren't so warm and humorous about it, rather bossy. But it never wounds or offends because the edge is taken off by her grin and your own knowledge of her integrity. Once when I was not well she took me home with her for a few days. Not wanting to be troublesome I made an effort to be helpful. She allowed just so much of it then turning on me she said, "Quit trying to be a Boy Scout. Be sick and enjoy it. Go sit down and get out from under my feet."

Occasionally she can be quite militant. Recently her town began an all-out campaign for city beautification. Pansy found herself on the central committee. This civic organization and that were charged with making the town beautiful and one of Pansy's pet projects was to make a tiny park out of a little valley just back of the town square. To her horror one morning she glanced out the window and saw men cutting down the trees. She lost no time getting on the telephone. "What," she yelped at the chairman, "are you cutting the trees for?"

"We thought we'd make a lawn and put benches around."

"What good would benches do without shade? You're ruining it! Don't you dare cut another tree and you get busy and put some more trees back! Just cut the bushes and clean up the trash. That's all it needs!"

"Pansy, how am I going to put trees back???"

"I don't know. That's your problem. But you put a tree back every place you've cut one!"

"Yes, ma'am."

A community takes that kind of bossiness only from someone so dearly loved that even her wails are highly regarded.

I think she is probably the most devoted follower John Wesley ever had. The Methodist Church couldn't run without her. Some time ago she was a delegate to some sort of state gathering of Methodist women. At one of the sessions she was poked from behind by the pencil of a diligent notetaker. "Did you get the name of that last speaker?"

Pansy shook her head. Pansy had neither pencil nor notebook.

"But what are you going to tell your group when you make your report?"

"I'm going to tell 'em I didn't bother with speakers' names and if they don't like the way I report a convention they can send somebody else next time."

I have since heard that there has never been a report quite like the one Pansy made. It set the whole church giggling and the whole town to talking. I can imagine what it was like. Earnest and serious about the important things but pricking gas balloons with deadly aim and taking no notice of non-essentials.

Her integrity is absolute. For Pansy there is no excuse for not doing, under any circumstances, what you know is right. During the depression she was, for a time, the referral agent for the WPA in her county. A man walked into her office one morning. "Magistrate John Doe said for you to give me a job."

Now, Magistrate John Doe was one of those at the top, who controlled, more or less, all WPA jobs. While Pansy had not sought the job of referral agent, had in fact been approached and asked to take it, still, to the average easy-morals person the magistrate's word would have been law. Not to Pansy. There was a procedure. And you had to meet certain requirements, qualify, before you got a job. Fire in her eyes she said to the man, "Oh, he did, did he? Well, you just march yourself right back to Magistrate John Doe and tell him you'll get a job if you qualify and not before! And you tell him, also, I'm running this office. If he doesn't like the way I'm running it he can have me fired but as long as I'm running it nobody can tell me how to do it!"

She got fired, all right. The magistrate owed a political debt to the man. The point is, she would have done precisely the same thing if she hadn't known where her next meal was coming from. There is no compromise in her on matters of principle.

In my opinion she is one of the best traditional artists painting in America today. There is a richness and depth to her work which is Rembrandt-like and makes the work of other artists look somehow pale and anemic. I believe she could show and sell anywhere, from any gallery, but it is typical of her that she loves her own town, doesn't want her life uprooted and disturbed, doesn't want to be famous, and whoever wants a Pansy Phillips painting, by golly, can just come to Greensburg, Kentucky, and buy it!

Her integrity in her painting is whole. When my daughter and her husband built a new home a few years ago I badly wanted to give them a Pansy Phillips canvas as a housewarming gift. I knew the size and type of painting Libby most wanted, a rather large one of the Jemez Mountains. Pansy shook her head. She had never seen the Jemez Mountains. Nor did she know the special place in her living room Libby would hang it. On an autumn vacation that year she and Russell wandered around the southwest a little, then went on to Santa Fe to spend a few days. Pansy spent nearly all of it sketching for the painting, so that Libby and I might choose — and studying Libby's room, seeing the mountains in it, pondering woods for the painting's framing. It is perfectly right, of course, flawless in its setting, grand and majestic but not overpowering, made even a little intimate with a water-ribboned arroyo in the foreground.

We learned that we were within three months of the same age and that we shared many of the same likes and dislikes. Both of us love gray, rainy days and dislike a bright, glaring sun. Both of us like water, to dream by, not to be out on. We both like best the old ways of life and admit cheerfully our inconsistency by enjoying all the luxuries of the modern. Old-fashioned, a little stately, we both have certain reserves. Deep emotions are kept private, even between us. We both dislike crowds, noise, cities, summer heat, and physical exertion. We are both indifferent housekeepers and neither of us suffers fools gladly. Our values touch and meet and run along the same streambed of temperament, instincts and sympathies. The friendship is free and easy and fully understood.

It has been one of those happy circumstances that our husbands enjoy each other also. Too often in married friendships there is a burr of irritation somewhere. To the best of my knowledge there is none in this foursome. Russell is tall, thin, beautifully groomed and a bundle of nerves. Mister G. is pudgy, always rumpled, but wholly nice and relaxed. Perhaps they offset each other, but at any rate they get along well and for this Pansy and I are very grateful.

We now brought Joe and Mitch to Pansy and Russell and they tucked them under their wings also and the core of the coterie was complete.

We usually gather at our house because we have usually lived in the country and we can make all the homemade music we like, hold a square dance or a singin', shoot target, go fishing, without committing a nuisance against the neighbors. Since the log house was finished, it's big enough and there are beds enough to sleep us all if necessary, and it sometimes is.

A lot of high jinks goes on when we are all together, for every last person in the group has a highly developed sense of fun and a tremendous capacity for enjoyment. There is one working painter, Pansy, and four of the rest of us are Sunday painters. Three of us write, two, Mister G. and myself, professionally, and Joe Covington dabbles. Two of the bachelors have fine, trained voices, and all of us can carry a tune. Mister G. is as good a "gittar" picker as ever came out of the Kentucky hills.

We make a lot of homemade music. We lean toward the raucous, brassy, belting rhythms of Bluegrass and country music and its kissing cousin, gospel singing. We are especially fond of the latter. The whole group, with the exception of myself, are middle-Kentucky, Bible-belt natives, and grew up on the Grand Ole Opry's country music and the shaped-note revival songs. Whatever their cultivated tastes they are not ashamed of their native music and retain a fondness for belting it out. Mister G., Pansy and Buddy Lowe have an endless repertoire. When we want to *listen* to music there is the record player with anything from Mozart to New Orleans jazz, but when we want to make music ourselves, Mister G. grabs his guitar and we take out after the Wabash Cannonball or the Crawdad Hole.

We early began the habit of having Thanksgiving together at one or another's home. It was at Bowling Green, now, that the long arm of circumstances or the hand of fate or whatever you want to call it reached out and touched a friendship again.

When she was only fifteen, Libby's most serious and steady boy friend was a lad a year or two older. Time and a change of residence separated them, then threw them together again when she was seventeen, when the relationship was resumed. Spinny Merwin became such a fixture in our home that I began to wonder if he might not become permanent. There was no alarm in the wonder because, in general, I was quite fond of him and had Libby chosen him to marry I should have been happy about it. For that matter, however, Libby never went with a boy I couldn't have taken into my heart. She was the most discriminating little miss that ever had dozens of devoted swains to choose from.

In the last year of their friendship, Spinny was at the University of Kentucky, his fraternity was Sigma Chi. Libby was at the University of Louisville and her sorority was Chi Omega. Vividly I recall a weekend she spent as his guest that year, specifically to attend the Sigma Chi dance. She came home pinned, distraught about it because she wasn't certain, dissolved into tears finally, boxed the pin and sent it back. "It was the moonlight, Mother," she said, "and the music. I don't want to be pinned yet."

Spinny took it philosophically. "I didn't much think she'd keep it," he said to me. "It was too good to be true." He grinned crookedly. "I'll just keep on trying."

And he did. He certainly did. He never entirely lost touch with her and all through the early years of the war, as she grew up and he grew up and finally went into the war himself, he wrote to her and came to remind her of himself as often as he could. Then she married Nash Hancock and we heard no more of Spinny Merwin.

We were wholly relaxed that Thanksgiving night after an excellent dinner in Joe's home when out of the happy comfort he suddenly said, "Hey, I spent last weekend in Louisville with a fraternity brother of mine and my roommate at the university for two years. Guess what? He knows you."

"He does?" I was only mildly interested.

"And there's more. He had a girl friend he used to rave about by the hour. Had a big, framed picture of her he used to keep on his dresser and talk to it and talk to it and talk to it." Joe grinned. "Her name was Libby!"

I sat up a little straighter. "*My* Libby?" But after all, I couldn't begin to count the boys who had had big, framed pictures of her. I know one who carried a photograph of her in the cockpit of his plane even after he knew she was married!

"Your Libby," Joe said. "Lord, I've heard that guy hold forth about Libby Moore by the hour, and I've heard you talk about your Libby. Never put two and two together until the other night. I don't know how it came up but the Gileses were mentioned and I said I knew you. This joker looked at me sort of funny and said, 'Do you know her daughter?'

"I said I didn't. I said she was coming this summer, however, and I was looking forward to meeting her.

"He said, 'Brother, you've not lived until you know Libby.'

"Good Lord, it hit me then — his Libby, your Libby, and my mouth dropped open a mile. He just grinned and said, 'Sure, they're the same.'"

Joe cocked his head to one side. "You know something? He said he tried for four long years to be your son-in-law."

"What was your fraternity?" I asked.

"Sigma Chi."

Of course — it had to be. "And your roommate was Spinny Merwin?"

He nodded.

There was the deepest pang of pain as the past rushed in, that lost and enchanted time when my daughter had been still my daughter, not yet a wife and mother. In a fanciful way I had the feeling that a circle had been completed, that it was meant that this man who when a much younger man had listened to another young man talk for hours about my daughter, dream aloud about her in hope and the anguish of losing her, who for two years had lived under her portrait eyes, should have become our dear friend. In a queer way it made sense to me, as if a pattern had been laid long ago and the pieces of our lives cut to it then later fitted together. I don't know how long I went away from my body, then — but it was long enough to remember . . . remember.

They were so beautiful together. He was tall and fair, with a scrubbed, clean look and he was a perfect foil for Libby's darkness. Sometimes when I watched them dancing together, his fair head laid against Libby's dark one, their movements so perfectly attuned it was as if some common current flowed between them, they were so incredibly beautiful, so vulnerably young, so naïvely sweet that my throat would knot and my stomach would tighten. If they could only always stay so unhurt. If they could just keep the crest of the wave. If they could just stay young and in love and gentle and tender. The knot and the tightness were because, of course, they could not. The hour and the age and the innocence could not be kept, could not be held. It must pass and life must have its way with them. Time and again when she was growing up it was heartbreaking to watch — one had a sense of God keep her all the time. But never so much as when she was fifteen.

They had the most wonderful times together. It was our first winter in Kentucky. There was a lot of snow and ice. We had snows in the southwest, too, but not very deep ones nor did they last very long. Neither Libby nor I had ever seen lakes and ponds and rivers frozen over for weeks at a time. A whole new field of winter sports opened up to Libby. She and Spinny went sledding, skiing, skating, she inexpertly but so merrily and gaily. More than once I heard her say she wished winter would never end.

It did, but when it did there was canoeing on the river, picnic suppers, hikes up in the hills, and when summer came there were long lazy days with swimming and more picnic suppers and long evenings for dancing. How *much* they danced, and how well and beautifully.

They went to the Senior Prom. It was the year Spinny

graduated from high school. The dance began at ten — rather late I thought. "But, Mom, we'll dance until two — then there is a swimming party, then breakfast."

"All *night?*" I was scandalized.

"Oh, *Mother!* There'll be chaperons!"

I didn't approve until I learned who they were and didn't wholly approve then. It seemed much too much of an affair for high school youngsters. But it was a tradition. I *couldn't*, especially when she was going with the class president, surely I *wouldn't* . . . and of course I didn't. She was allowed to go, and there was a new evening dress, and a new swimsuit.

I remember how she came in at dawn — her swimsuit still dripping, her hair wet, circles of sleeplessness under her eyes but stars shining from them. "Fun?" I asked.

"Wonderful," she said, tumbling into bed, "simply wonderful!" and she was instantly asleep.

Sometimes, remembering, I think *just* about her evening dresses, for almost each one recalls a special time. There were dozens, none of them expensive, for I was nimble with a thimble and she was original and creative and had a sure instinct for what was right for herself. We whipped one up for her at the drop of a hat, usually of cotton, usually white, for white — and no one knew better than she how much — set off her dark beauty strikingly. The one for Spinny's prom was white organdy, deceptively demure until the eye found the embroidered ruffle at her hips from which the fulness of the skirt fell away.

There was a blue denim, for a hayride dance. It had red bandanna shoulder straps and a clever hip pocket from which another bandanna dangled. And there was a peppermint stripe with scads of ruffles. What was that one for? Oh, yes — to lead the Grand March at the K.M.I. Seniors' ball. Another class president, at Kentucky Military Institute this time. I remember the dress cost precisely three dollars!

There were of course moirés and taffetas and organzas, too. My family were good about sending materials, or evening dresses of their own which I could remake. Though she had so many, we didn't spend much on her evening dresses. We hoarded our pennies, rather, for those really lovely things like cashmere sweaters and Italian silk shirts and tweeds. By the time she was sixteen we were of a size to share everything but skirts and shoes. I wore my skirts a little too long and my feet were narrower and smaller. Thus what seemed extravagance was really not — sweaters, shirts, jackets and topcoats did for two.

For Commencement week when she herself graduated from high school, she bought perhaps the most expensive evening gown she has ever had out of gift money. It was a sheer black organza over flesh taffeta, the skirt extremely full and standing out as if it had hoops. She wore gold hoops in her ears with it, and gold bangles on her arms and a fall of gold necklace around her throat. When I dressed Savanna for the colonel's ball at old Fort Gibson, in the book of the same name, *Savanna*, I remembered Libby's gold bangles and Libby's gold hoops. Indeed, I could not have helped it, for Libby is all through the character of Savanna! The same independence, the same "by myself" attitude, the same come-a-cropper and pick-myself-up again fortitude, the same color and flair and life and gypsy vividness. Libby was sweeter and gentler and less self-centered, but she provided a form on which I could drape a pioneer character.

She wore the black organza for several years after she was

married . . . wore it, in fact, until she grew heavier after having three babies and had sadly to lay it away. There was a tear for it, which she shook away. It had seen so many good times. She wrote me about it. "Mother, thank you for my girlhood. It was the most wonderful any daughter ever had. Nobody ever, ever had more fun, or more happiness, or more lovely things to remember."

Well, then — peace.

I came back into my body and joined again these good, good friends, central in my own life and in life's inexplicable ways edged, too, into my daughter's — the fabric and color of Pansy's textures on her walls, and the fabric and color of Pansy's character stretched in friendship beyond the mother to the daughter ever after. Joe Covington's knowledge of a boy's love for her which, in its telling, may have given him a knowledge unknown to me. Mitchell's months in the bootheel of Italy in the same air command as her husband. Woven all around me was her nearness, through them as well as my memories.

They sensed where I had been and somebody lifted a glass. "To Libby!"

Chapter 13
Henry and Honey

Mrs. G. has mentioned some of our two-legged friends but
we also have, and have had, a number of four-legged ones
I'd like to talk about. Dogs have been very much a part of
our life since a few months after we were married.

We began with Honey. It was 1946. We lived in Louisville and one winter of the city drove the country boy in
me to the desperate need of a place to rest on weekends.
We bought a few square yards of land and an old log cabin
on Bullitt's Lick, some seventeen miles from downtown

Louisville. We spent a happy spring taking the cabin down and rebuilding it into a snug, habitable structure. We enjoyed our weekends there so much that when summer came we moved to the cabin for the hot months and commuted to the city and our work.

Now the country and a dog go together as companionably as ham and eggs, so it was during that summer that we reached the conclusion we must have a dog. Since in my opinion the only place to find a good honest dog is Adair County, we crawled into our 1939 Oldsmobile and pointed her nose in that direction.

We talked to my dad, a dog-knowing man if there ever was one. "What kind of dog you want?" he asked.

We had no preferences. Just a good dog.

He pondered a minute or two, then said he knew some people down in the valley that were moving to Cincinnati. He had heard they had a dog they were right fond of and since they couldn't take it to the city they wanted to find a good home for it. "Pretty little dog," Dad said. He whittled a stroke or two, then added flatly, "female, though."

Bristling defensively, Mrs. G. said, "What difference does that make? There have to be both kinds and to refuse a dog because she's a she . . ."

My dad smiled. "Think you'd like to see her, son?"

"What is she? Hound?"

"No. She's part collie, part shepherd."

In Adair County we call that mixture "short-nosed collie," and it's a good crossbreed. Such a dog usually is steady, intelligent, trainable and more often than not has a good nose. My dad would never have a bitch. Too much trouble, he said. So I had no experience to guide me but I thought

I could handle the situations as they arose. It would, I believed, require only a reasonable amount of watchfulness
twice a year, a three-week restriction to quarters for the
dog, and all would be well. I learned differently. I learned,
for eleven years, a considerable amount more than I wanted
to learn about the resourcefulness of dogs in the intensity of
love. Time and again we were urged and advised by well-
meaning people to have her spayed. We wouldn't have done
it for the world. Honey had a right to be herself, her whole
self, for all the years of her life. We didn't mind her having
pups once a year, and we never once bred her. We let her
do her own choosing. But we thought twice a year was a
little much, and too hard on her. And that was when we
had trouble.

But all of that was in the future. At the moment I said it
wouldn't hurt to look at her. "Fine," my dad said, "come
down again next weekend and I'll have her here."

If we had expected to look her over and make a rational
decision, it was the most mistaken expectation ever harbored.
One look, and we were committed. There was no decision
to make. She was our dog and no mistaking it. She was
beautiful, with an amber coat of silky hair like pure honey,
only a few splashes of clean white on her. Her eyes were
amber, too, and clear and bright and shining. We loved her
at once and because of her coloring named her on the spot
— Honey.

She fell for us as hard as we fell for her. She came straight
to us, nosed us, pranced a little, then fell to romping with us.
We melted and there was never a time, for eleven long
years, when Honey didn't own us heart and soul. We didn't
give her a good home. She simply took over and ran our

home and ran our lives for all those years. Somehow I think she sensed that we were the people she had been looking for. In fact, I guessed later that she had our number from the beginning. If her thoughts could have been translated, I believe they would have gone like this: "I've been looking for these two people all my life. Finally I've found them. And these two I can handle with a wag of my tail. I just feel it in my bones. I'm gonna *love* owning these two people." And that's the way it was. Any shift, move, or trip we made thereafter, Honey and her comfort had to be considered first.

She was eleven months old when she came to us and we took her from Adair County to the cabin on Bullitt's Lick. She loved riding in the car. She loved it on that trip. At first she was greatly fascinated by all the cars we met. She watched eagerly ahead for a car, then as it passed she would stand up in the back window and watch it until it was out of sight behind us, woofing and barking a little as if she, personally, had routed it. For fully fifty of the hundred miles she occupied herself thus, then she tired of it and just sat back and rode.

All her life she loved to ride, and she liked best to stand in the car window with her front legs and head outside and grab at bushes and limbs as we drove along the narrow country roads. And she would grab at anything in reach. We couldn't teach her that some of the limbs had thorns. We have seen her latch onto big blackberry vines and strip the top clean of leaves, scratching her mouth until it bled. She would shake her head and spit out the briars, then grab the next bush that came within reach. When we came to Adair County to live she quickly learned all the roads we traveled and knew every spot that had overhanging limbs and bushes.

She particularly loved the mile and a half between our house and my dad's. It had half a dozen fine grabbing spots on it, and she would peer excitedly ahead, her tail in violent agitation, strained forward until we sometimes wondered how she kept her balance. But she only cared for this sport in the spring and summer when there was full foliage. She had no interest in bare limbs. She was perfectly content to ride in stately dignity on the back seat with the car windows rolled up when the leaves fell.

She was not a trick dog, because we never tried to teach her any. She was intelligent enough to have learned any tricks you wanted to teach her, but we don't like performing dogs. I want a dog trained. I want him to know what Get out, Lie down, Let's go, Be quiet, and Stay, mean. That's all I ask. Trick dogs have lost their dignity, it seems to me. And don't think dogs don't have a fine sense of dignity, or that they can't be embarrassed when losing it.

Honey was chasing a bird once, after a rainy morning. She lost her footing and did a dive, sliding a good distance on her nose in the mud. Mrs. G. and I thought it hilarious and whooped loudly. Honey picked herself up and swung a few yards away, refused to look at us, stood nobly and proudly gazing into the distance, recovering as best she could her lost dignity. She was so embarrassed and humiliated that she trembled. We were ashamed. We should have known better. We approached her with apologies and soft words, but she would have none of us, saying as plainly as possible with her attitude, "You laughed at me! Sure, it was funny. But gentle people don't laugh when there's an accident. Gentle people *know* how embarrassing it is." We crept into the house, embarrassed ourselves beyond measure, fully rebuked for our rudeness. With great generosity she forgave us eventually, but we never forgot again.

She was still a pup in many ways that first year we had her, and like most young dogs she had a favorite plaything, but I believe hers was a little unusual. Shortly after we brought her to the cabin on Bullitt's Lick, Mrs. G. began having to sweep a knotty little stump of cedar off the front steps every morning. "What *is* this?" she asked, handing it to me. "It's here on the steps every day."

I examined it and found it toothmarked. "Whatever it is," I said, "it's Honey's. She's been gnawing it."

Thereafter it was left unmolested on the steps. Then one morning we saw her playing with it. She would toss it in the air and chase it for a while, then lie down with it between her paws and chew on it. Mrs. G. was of the opinion she was cutting teeth and wanted something hard to relieve the pressure. Maybe. I suppose dogs cutting teeth aren't very different from babies, at that. But when she had gnawed it down to a splintery nub I was afraid she would choke on a sliver or stick one in her gums. I tossed the nubbin into a thicket of briars on the creek bank and thought that would be the end of it. Not so. It was right back on the front steps the next morning. A day or two later I tried again to get rid of it. I buried it. But she unearthed it and I gave up. She chewed on that little red nubbin until it was gone, just chewed away.

Out of sheer physical energy she chased everything that moved — a leaf blowing across the yard, hoptoads, terrapins, chickens — when she was young. The wild life on Bullitt's Lick had a hard time of it her first year there. Not that she ever caught or killed anything, but if it moved it was to chase.

And the birds especially fascinated her. There were a good many birds in the small pine forest that surrounded the cabin and in the thickets along the creek. In no sense a bird dog, when she flushed a covey of quails she simply scattered them to the four winds and the whir-r-r and bulletlike speed with which a woodcock got up never ceased to astonish her.

We were at the supper table one evening, still light enough to see but twilight coming on, when we heard Honey barking. I listened. It had a new sound in it. "By george," I said, shoving back from the table, "she's barking treed!"

We flew to the creek bank where she was squatted under a big elm. She was very excited and while she welcomed us she didn't leave her place. She had treed and her job was to stay put until I took over the situation, until I fired the shot and dropped the game. "What have you got, Honey? What you got up there?" My guess was possum.

She eased off a little, knowing I was in charge now. I circled the tree, stopped short and began laughing. I called to Mrs. G. "Come here and see what she's treed."

In the crotch of the tree was a small owl, undisturbed and unruffled at being treed by Honey. As we watched him he lifted his wings slowly, blinked, then rose in the air and drifted away. Honey watched him in amazement, then in frantic despair. She gave chase but he disappeared across the creek. She returned to me and her disgust was plain. "Idiot! You let him get away!" I tried to explain but she wanted nothing to do with such a bumbling fool. Nose and tail both high she parted company with me.

She had three beautiful male pups that first year, all, naturally, of very uncertain pedigree. But they thrived and she was an excellent mother. When they were about two months old we took the finest one to Adair County as a gift for my youngest brother. We left Honey, with the others, in the toolshed which had been converted into a home for them.

We got back to the cabin late on Sunday afternoon and while Honey came to meet us there were no pups with her. The toolshed door was always left ajar so Honey could nose it open and take the pups for a walk and where they went she went also, or perhaps it was the other way round. We looked around the yard for them, but when we went in the cabin we knew we'd never find them. They had been stolen, for the cabin had been broken into. The furniture was all piled helter-skelter, the beds turned upside down and ripped apart, even some pictures had been taken down and ripped in half. Evidently money or something valuable had been the object of search and then perhaps anger at not finding anything had caused the thieves to turn vandals. But outside of the pups, a fine and expensive compass was the only thing we missed. It probably turned up later in some pawnshop in the city. We wouldn't have felt so disconsolate about the pups if we could have believed they would have good homes, but the kind of people who destroyed property weren't exactly the kind to be good to dogs. We have wondered many times about the pups but we never did learn where they went or what happened to them.

It was shortly after this that we bought the forty-acre farm in Adair County and moved to the country permanently.

Honey was in heaven, for by now she was beginning to hunt. I took her out with a gun and watched her. On that first trip she treed three squirrels and I was excited because she treed by sight. When she barked "treed" there was never any mistake about it, she had a squirrel. It might be a den tree and I might not get a shot, but she had seen a squirrel climb the tree. She didn't take it lightly when I called her away without firing, either. She had done her part, she seemed to say, now why hadn't I done mine? Occasionally she would have two in a tree. I would shoot one and start moving on. But when she barked up the tree again, there was always another squirrel and she knew it.

There was a special urgency in her voice from the edge of the field back of the house one morning. I grabbed the rifle and went to investigate. Up a small oak snag she was barking at a groundhog — the biggest one I ever saw. He was almost as big as Honey. Well, we didn't have anything the old fellow could bother much, so I hesitated to shoot him. We sort of live by that code — if you won't bother us, we won't bother you — and we apply it to humans as well as animals. But Honey was frantic, saying, "Come on, Man, shoot the varmint out. This is *our* place, you know."

So I laid the rifle down and found a long pole. I saw that when he hit the ground all he had to do was roll over a couple of times and he could duck into a big den and safety. Inexperienced as Honey was, I thought she wouldn't touch the old boy.

I eased one end of the pole up. The groundhog bit chunks out of it and snapped his teeth at me. I shoved hard and he fell and, according to my figuring, should have rolled downhill to safety. Not so. No sooner did he hit the ground than Honey had him by the scruff of the neck and she backed him uphill fast. *She* knew the den was there, too, and she got him away from it.

In amazement I watched her. She worked her mouth-hold back to just behind his shoulders, then pushed the old chuck into the ground while she pressed and bit and pressed and bit. Soon she let go and backed off, growling. I waited for him to get up and move away. That chuck didn't move a muscle. He was, as we say, deader than four o'clock. Honey pranced to the house in front of me, saying plainly, "There. That'll teach him to trespass. We sure got rid of him, didn't we? And I'll bet you didn't think I could do it."

By george, I *didn't* think she could do it!

She was a fairly good rabbit dog and could have been coached into being an excellent one, but it wasn't her first love. The deep woods, this man who belonged to her, the gun and a bushy-tail, were the things she loved most. Her heart was in her eyes when I picked up the gun. She always believed we were headed for the woods. If, instead, I took the path to the meadow and the thickets, the pride went out of her ears and tail and her eyes were disappointed. "Rabbits! For heaven's sake, *why* do you want to fool with those things? What's there about hunting rabbits? They just run in circles."

So they do, I told her, but they're pretty good eating occasionally.

I tried never to let her down when she treed. If a man has got a good dog he has to go to some trouble to keep it good and if you let a good squirrel or coon dog down too many times he'll quit treeing. It's as if he thought, why bother. I have got up at three o'clock in the morning, dressed and clambered down that long steep hollow in front of our house when she barked "treed," because Honey would stay there until I came, whether it was an hour, a day, or a week. She'd stay there and starve to death or freeze. You just don't disappoint a dog that faithful, and you get to her as fast as you can. When she was so old and crippled with rheumatism that she had to be helped to her feet that spark would still come in her eyes and her tail would still wag when I picked up the gun. It nearly broke our hearts and I quit hunting until she died. I couldn't go and leave her behind.

For quite a while Honey's pups were the only dogs in our life. We usually gave them away, and there were always plenty of takers, but occasionally there would be such an appealing little fellow that we couldn't part with him. At one time or another we have had as many as three until a lengthy trip, extended over months perhaps, would make us have to give them away.

Such a one was Rusty, who grew to manhood, made a good hunting dog, a friendly companion, and a fine watchdog. He had only one fault. He chased cars and I could never break him of it. It was his undoing.

In the spring of 1953 road crews were putting gravel on the far end of our ridge road and the gravel trucks went barreling by all day long. Mrs. G. was in Santa Fe that spring standing watch over our grandsons while her daughter was hospitalized for surgery. I had business in town one morning and when I came home Rusty was nowhere to be found. He wouldn't come, as he always did, when I called, nor could I hear him barking down the hollow. With a sinking heart I thought of the gravel trucks. Their noise and speed fascinated Rusty and he never gave up trying to catch one. I went walking up the road and finally found him. It made me sick at my stomach and I hoped he had been killed instantly. I hoped that, in my absence to comfort, he had not lain in the ditch in pain as he died. I stroked his thick pelt and said goodbye to him and was glad Mrs. G. was not there.

Under a big cherry tree in one corner of the yard I buried him. I then smoothed the soil down and traced a big R over him and sowed a handful of grass seed in the outline. For several years a big green grassy R stood out plainly, then the grass spread and the R, like Rusty, was no more.

Another of her pups we kept was a black and white shorthair. His father must have been a hound. He was the liveliest pup I have ever seen. From the time he could stand and walk at all he was running and jumping at anything that moved. And from the start he loved to jump over things. He sailed over the rail fence that enclosed the front yard the way a horse takes a jump. So we named him Jumper. Instead of running down a hillside, he jumped down it. Open the door and he jumped in the house.

He grew into a huge dog, twice as big as Honey. He was lovable but I have to admit he was short on sense. He never did learn how to hunt. He'd get up a rabbit, run it out of sight, and the hunt was over as far as he was concerned. He'd stand and watch a squirrel run up a tree, cock his head to one side, turn around and walk off and leave it. As far as Jumper was concerned a rabbit was gone when it was out of sight and a squirrel was no further problem when it had climbed a tree. And he never barked at anything.

He went along when Honey and I went squirrel hunting but he let her do all the treeing. He never left my side. And he would never nose or sniff a dead squirrel when I had shot. But when he got home, he was in his element. Whatever game I killed I usually put on top of a huge stump in the back yard to clean. This was Jumper's clue to leap up beside it and lie there, guarding the game until I was ready to clean it.

He died young. Something went wrong, we never knew

what, for one day he was healthy and full of life. The next morning I found him lying under the eave of the house, in convulsions. It takes a long time to forget a big old awkward pet such as Jumper was.

Our first dog not related to Honey was Ring. We still have him. He must be nearly eight years old now. He was given to us by a neighbor when he was three months old. For a long time I had been wanting a good coon hound and Ring was the son of one of the best. He was blackish-brown with a white ring around his neck, so his name was inevitable.

He was slightly infected with mange when I brought him home, so I gave him a bath of used motor oil mixed with sulphur. He didn't look like much for a few days but the mange was cured and when he had slicked off he was as glossy as any pup we'd ever had.

On Thanksgiving day of that year, still less than a year old, Ring ran his first rabbit. My dad and I always hunt together on Thanksgiving day and we took Ring along with Honey that day just to see what he *might* do. He got up the first rabbit we saw and although we didn't get a shot because it ran into a den, he was staying with it right on around.

Jumper was still with us when we got Ring and they had some great romps together which were funny to watch. It was like seeing an elephant and a Shetland colt playing together.

But Honey was the boss. We had to feed each dog in his own feeding pan because Honey wouldn't allow the two young dogs to touch a bite of food otherwise. We have seen her guard one small piece of bread for half a day, baring her teeth and growling when either pup approached. They learned very early, too, to respect her rank in the family.

That first winter, Honey jumped most of the rabbits but when they took to a briar patch she would bounce up a few times and let Ring take over. She would then wait with me for the rabbit to come around. In time Ring became, and still is, the best rabbit dog in these parts. He is faster and more sure, even, than beagles.

I've killed many a squirrel with him, too, although he couldn't be classified as an expert squirreler. As long as he's trailing he's on firm ground, but when a squirrel trees, Ring loses his authority. And he admits it. He will bark up first one tree then another, telling me, "You find him, Boss. He's in one of these trees but I'm not dead sure which."

As long as Honey lived and hunted, I didn't need another squirrel dog, and for a few years I was just about the best-fixed hunter north of Green River. I had the best squirrel dog in these parts in Honey, and in Ring I had the best rabbit dog. Who could ask for more?

They were completely different in disposition and temperament. Honey rarely needed a scolding, but on the few occasions she did, she took it in high dudgeon. She never quailed or let her tail droop. She looked you straight in the eye as if to say, "Who do you think you are, scolding *me!*" One sharp word was enough to send Ring wailing under the floor. His feelings were so tender that the raised voice, whether speaking to him or not, made him droop and creep away. I never hit him but once, with a rolled newspaper at that. It made him sick and it took half a day to coax him out from under the porch and be friends again.

Ring is a long story. I write a weekly column for the *Adair County News* and every so often Ring is the subject. Everybody in the county knows him. Once the *Courier-Journal* magazine had an article about dogs in which the writer voiced the opinion that the day of the old-time dogs had passed. He said that nowadays they are all high bred and specialized; there were no more old Rovers or Neros or Rattlers or Rings. We quickly repudiated the idea by letter and were immediately asked to send a picture of our Ring. A few weeks later Ring made the front pages of the magazine section and came to have a wider fame. Strangers at our door, if they are Kentuckians, are likely to ask to see Ring and he has his picture taken pretty often, too.

Our newest dog is a beagle pup. He was given to us in April, 1962, and was three months old at the time. Because he is the spitten image of our old Rusty, his name is Rusty II. Hunters have told me he is a twelve-inch beagle. I didn't know they came in inches but it seems they do. There is another breed of sixteen-inch beagles and for all I know there may be more. The more inches, the bigger the beagle, as I understand it.

I have high hopes of Rusty II, although I'm not sure yet of what. He may turn out to be a retriever, for at his present age, five months, he retrieves every old rag, bag, sack or bottle he can find in the dump pit and brings it to the back porch. This is annoying, but it's not fatal. A little worse is his habit of latching onto anything put down for a few minutes — such as a pair of work gloves, a small tool, a lady's handbag, or even the leaf rake. These things, too, must be carried to the back porch. He has staked out the back porch as his own safety deposit box. When Pansy Phillips was doing some sketches for this book, she laid her sketching pad on a yard table and went inside the house for a few minutes. She had heart failure when she went back out. Rusty II was just disappearing around the corner of the porch, head high, her sketch pad in his mouth. She did a little retrieving herself and found no great damage done. He had mouthed several sketches, chewed the corner of one, but none of them were hopelessly ruined.

We will be glad, however, when his affinity for dead things is behind him. It is disconcerting to step outside and be greeted by a decomposed fish, frog, squirrel, rabbit, or cat. The episode of the cat almost caused us to leave home for a week. And we began to believe he was psychic about finding it. It was in a bad enough state when he lugged it home the first time. It took two days and much spraying to rid the porch of the odor. I buried the remains. Several days later he had proudly brought it home again. Age had added nothing to it but a riper odor. Again I buried it; this time very far from the house. A week went by before Rusty found it, but find it he did. This time I burned the carcass in the dump pit, which I should have had sense enough to do in the beginning. I hope this means his rabbit nose will be as good as his dead-cat nose.

On the other hand, Rusty may well become a water dog. He is a young hound who really loves water. When I fish, I usually do a lot of wading. Rusty likes to stay right with me. The trouble is that while I wade, Rusty has to swim. He has a lot of staying power, but eventually he is exhausted. When I hear him panting, it's time to pick him up and take him ashore. And then as soon as he has rested a while he's right back out in the middle of the river again.

Our farm pond is fairly sizable and it's well stocked with game fish. Occasionally I cast a few surface plugs at the pond instead of going to the river. Twilight was sending me home one evening and I called Rusty, "Let's go." He was across the pond from me and I expected him to run around the end. Not Rusty. The shortest way was straight across the water and straight across the water he came.

And he doesn't mind water over his head. In fact, he does a weird sort of diving act. Swimming along he'll suddenly dive for a pebble or a crawfish or something shiny on the bottom. On a hot day he likes to plunge in the river head first and swim with his head under water. I don't know; maybe he's going to be a skin diver.

We only have Ring and Rusty II, now. Honey never got to live in the log house. We lost her in November of 1957. She had been suffering from rheumatism all that year, groaning with the effort it required to get up when she was lying down. It was Mrs. G. who noticed one morning that her mammary glands were swollen as if she were going to have pups. We knew that was impossible. We had taken care to protect her for several years because of her rheumatism. We took her to the vet, who examined her in our presence. "She has a mammary tumor," he said. "It will have to be excised."

He persuaded us not to stay. It was a Saturday and he promised to operate that same day. "Come back Monday," he said, "and perhaps you can take her home."

We had a restless Sunday and perhaps if there were telephone service in our part of the county we would have called to see how she was. There being none we sweated it out, but we were at the hospital bright and early Monday morning.

We have not harbored resentment. We know, under the circumstances, unable to reach us except by making a long trip out to our house, that the man had a difficult decision to make and made it for the best as he saw it. The tumor had been so extensive that it could not be excised without crippling her, without leaving her in such a condition that she could not walk without pain, nor could it be fully excised without leaving her only a few months of life. He thought it best, while she was under the anesthetic, simply to put her away. Maybe so. Maybe so. But I would have liked to see her again. And if I had known what had to be, I think I would have taken the gun so that she could go to sleep looking at the things she loved most in her world — the man she owned and his gun.

We love Ring and Rusty, but they don't own us the way Honey did. What a man feels for a dog like Honey is a little like his feeling for his wife, and perhaps it only comes once in a lifetime. I expect to have many a good hunt with Ring yet, and I expect to have many a fine hunt with the beagle, but I'll tell you something unashamed. I don't expect ever again to have the kind of hunts I had with Honey, the heart-lifting joy of the two of us, young together and tireless and quick and eager. I am not the man I was and they are not the dog she was. No. That will not happen again.

But I remember Honey . . .

Chapter 14
The Fountain of Youth Isn't There

THE WINTER marched on, our house continuing topless. We had a sad, wet Christmas.

One of our burdens since May had been the illness of Mister G.'s mother. When a spring cold lingered on interminably with a rattle, wheezy cough, and pains in her chest and side, we sped her to the doctor who probed and punched, questioned and X-rayed, and then pronounced the fearful word "Tuberculosis." Arrangements were quickly made for her to enter a sanatorium. The summer and the autumn had passed and while the disease was arrested the complete cure was fretfully delayed. She was always in our hearts and minds, for she loathed every second of her imprisonment in that gaunt place. We loathed it for her, but we wanted her well and hearty and worriless when she returned eventually.

She was given a week of home leave at Christmas and we gathered her up, with the other members of Mister G.'s family at home, for a feast of sorts. It was a dreary attempt, though the tree sparkled bravely and colored bulbs framing the doorway did their best to lend festivity. Mister G.'s mother could not be merry knowing she must return to her hospital room and we could not be merry with a new and catastrophic knowledge lying on our hearts.

We had been, we believed, very wise and foresighted when we began building our house. A writer's income is unpredictable and it comes in heavy or light batches to him twice a year when royalties are paid. For that reason, and because you never know ahead what a given book will earn, these particular writers don't go in debt very much. We have cash in hand before we proceed. We did not begin building our house until there was a fatter bank account than usual and the promise of more of the same.

Hannah Fowler was the book, we decided when it was selected for a richer than usual book club contract, to build our house. What seemed to us a huge book club check had come to us early in 1957. Another of like size, we knew, could be expected the following year for *The Believers.* We crowed over our riches. We could easily build our house and have scads of money left over! Thus fortified, we embarked.

To our utter horror the book club money for *The Believers* was paid over to us in December of 1957, making two wealthy book club payments fall within one calendar year! This sent our income sky high and income tax calculations became astronomical.

With visions of our lovely dollars flying out the window toward the Treasury Department in Washington, I scurried to my lawyer who sent me on to a tax accountant. Vaguely I knew there were situations with actors and artists and musicians and writers when income could be spread over several years. How many, I had no idea, or how much one's income had to be. Ours had contained no such problems before!

"Yes," the accountant said, "there are such provisions." It seemed he had stayed up half the night studying the tax laws and he cited test cases in which brave writers had gone into court so that a tax break might accrue to others in similar situations. "They are hedged about, however," he continued, "with limitations. If it has taken you as much as three years to write either of these books, and if your income during those three years was not more than such-and-such a percent of the cash payments you have received this year, then the total may be spread over the three years."

My heart sank. It never takes me three years to write a book. If the time for research were included I still would have no idea how long it takes, for I never stop doing research. Wherever I go and whatever I do, I am soaking up material, reading, studying and making notes. There is no place on the face of the earth whose history isn't interesting to me, and about which I don't want to know. It's practically endless, my research. But I couldn't truthfully say I had set about writing either *Hannah Fowler* or *The Believers* as long as three years before their completion. And there was no isolating the time for special research for it was all part and parcel of the whole. When did I get the idea for *Hannah Fowler?* Ten years before when I first read the story of

Jenny Wiley? Or when my editor said, "You ought to do a book about a pioneer woman." And how long ago was that?

Besides, it was all rhetorical anyhow. Not since my first royalty check has my income fallen below a certain comfortable figure. During the three years in question it had been quite adequate. The accountant grinned at me. "I see nothing for you to do but pay off. I know it's going to hurt you badly this year, but I can't see any alternative. And my own experience has been that when I try to foresee and spread income I end up worse off than if I just let the chips fall where they will. Perhaps next year will make up for it," he added.

"Not," I said grimly, "unless I starve to death."

Nothing could make up for that check we had to write to the Director of Internal Revenue. It amounted, almost, to the entire sum paid to me by the book club for *The Believers*. I felt quite bitter. I told myself and I told Mister G. and I told anybody else who would listen that in effect I had simply written one book for the United States government. And for months I was quite critical of the way tax money was being spent. I felt that my own taxes that year had gone a long way toward supporting this or that colonel in the army, or this or that bureaucrat, or so many miles of federal highways, or that I had singlehandedly and alone moved dozens of wives and children to Europe to be with their husbands and fathers in the service. Everytime I paid toll on Kentucky's new toll road I quarreled. "I know I built a mile of it," I said.

Mister G. reminded me the road was said to have cost a million dollars per mile. "Then I built an inch," I declared, "and I want to ride on it free!"

"Take it up with the President," he advised.

It had been horrifying to learn, also, as we made out our tax return, that Mister G.'s tiny salary at the *Adair County News*, just a stipend really because he worked more for the love of the work than the salary, was nothing but another tax load. That small figure overlapped us and sent us into a higher bracket. The bracket we were already in was astronomical enough we thought, but there it was. And the resulting tax addition was more than Mister G.'s salary for the year!

In complete disgust he quit. Things had come, he said bitterly, to a fine pass when a man had to pay the government to work! Our tax problems in 1958 almost made Republicans of us, I can assure you.

And now, as the year turned, not only was the weather against us but we had to begin pinching pennies. All that beautiful *Believers* money was salted down, I firmly believed, at Fort Knox, and we had only a few thousands left of the *Hannah Fowler* money. I moaned we'd be lucky if we finished the house at all and misquoted Robert Frost, "Something there is that doesn't love a house . . ." We must, I said, give up all ideas of luxury or even much beauty in trim and tile, flooring and carpeting and fixtures. We must shop for the cheapest things we could find and make do with them.

It was heartbreaking to take a pencil and cross out brutally and ruthlessly all the extras we might have had, all the small fine touches, unusual and pretty and our own, and substitute for them the banal and the trite and the cheap. We weren't even able to substitute for some of them, we had to do without completely. Such as proper insulation and a

central heating system. Such as the finished and elegant bedroom I had designed, with its cedar-lined walk-in closet and
dressing room. Such as the second bath. We had to adopt
as our goal not much more than the logs chinked and mor-
tared and the roof finally in place.

We sloshed through a dark and gloomy January. Certain
now that before this house was completed we would be
eating hamburgers and beans we made a budget, something
we rarely do and loathe when we must. Neither of us is
budget minded. We don't think we are extravagant people
but we hate to peer through the bars of dollars and cents at
the world. Better managers than we would have done more
with the money the books have made, probably; but few
people would have had a better time with it! We like to say
at breakfast, let's go to Fayetteville, or let's go to Santa Fe,
or let's go to the mountains, or let's go to the Breaks of the
Sandy, and within an hour be on our way. But besides that,
we are dedicated believers in living right here at home just
as comfortably and handsomely as the bank account will
allow. We don't really throw money around. But neither
do we try to preserve it for posterity. Nobody ever had to
tell us you can't take it with you. We already knew that in
our bones, and we mean to make this one and only time
granted to us on this earth memorable.

But now, we said, we mustn't spend a dime that isn't
necessary. We mustn't give parties. We mustn't buy bourbon. We mustn't buy sirloin and mushrooms and straw-
berries. We mustn't take any trips. "We mustn't live,"
Mister G. groaned.

Having promised ourselves to take no trips, we now
threw commonsense to the winds and went gypsying to
Florida with Pansy and Russell.

We came home as brown as Indians and road weary, and more in love than ever, in spite of snow and ice, with our own Kentucky landscape.

We came home, too, to late February and, for a change, to some fair weather. Spring does come at last. My weather calendar, kept for the past several years, shows that nearly always in February there are ten days or two weeks of unseasonably warm, balmy weather. Now we made the best possible use of it. We hired an enormous crew of men once more and in three days that impossible roof was put in place. I heaved a sigh of exquisite relief. I had begun to have an uneasy feeling it would never be accomplished. Nothing, now, could prevent progress from being made.

And work did seem to march. The chinks between the logs were sealed, the chimney was finished, the flooring was laid and sanded and varnished and polished. Windows were installed and the panes were cleaned and left speckless and glistening. Paneling in the middle section went up on the walls and ceilings and was painted a soft creamy white. And Joe Spires wrought a miracle and wired the house.

Joe was no electrician but we believed so strongly in his genius that it never occurred to us to get a real electrician. So Joe, grinning, tackled it.

We wanted no danger of fire from faulty wiring so early we had determined to use heavy duty wiring throughout. A master switch was installed and each room was put on its own circuit. A blown fuse never darkens but one room of our house. With as many as eight outlets, two switches, and a central fixture in some of the rooms, Joe's job was intricate and difficult. I have an unerasable memory of watching him trace painfully over and over and over again each circuit and every length of wire, each switch and outlet and fixture.

The wiring had to show in the log rooms naturally, and while Joe minded and made it as neat as possible, I couldn't have cared less. It seemed fine enough to me. He did sink the switches and outlets into the logs, however, and if he had had his way all the wiring would have been boxed into concealment. He never liked to leave rough edges on his work.

He accomplished miracles with the light fixtures, also. From old Mexico my daughter had sent us two quaint pieces which I wanted wired and made into fixtures, one for the bath — a six-pointed star — and one for the entrance hall — a tin lantern. Joe did it and they still hang and work today.

In the dining room I wanted an ancient gas chandelier made of brass with china shades. It had hung in the fishing camp and I was fond of it. Joe converted it to electricity and hung it precisely where I wanted it.

When it was all done the inspector came out from the utility company. He kept going around looking and testing and saying, "Beautiful. Beautiful. A beautiful job of wiring." We had known it would be, but Joe blushed a little.

Not only in those days but always I don't know what we should have done without Joe Spires. From the day we came to Adair County he has been not only our friend but our savior, making our old cars run, mending leaks in our roofs, building our porches, fixing our lawn mowers, doing all things and all things well. I don't know what we would do without him today. He grows our tobacco for us, and makes our vegetable garden ready for planting, and plows it. When we go away for a few months he sometimes moves his family into our house the better to care for it for us. If it is a trip of only a few weeks he comes daily to feed the

dogs and cats and to inspect the house. He tests the locks
and the windows and goes through to make sure everything
is in place and undisturbed, no sudden leaks, no gas escaping,
no frozen pipes. I may be wrong but I think in addition
to being fond of us, he loves this old house too. He ought to,
for he put a lot of himself into it.

He is a little younger than Mister G. but they were in
school together and they were young men together. They
share many memories and their friendship is fast. But I am
hurt sometimes by Joe. His nerve ends are too close to the
skin and he is too hurt by what he sees and feels and senses
and loves and loses. He sees all the little things other eyes
miss and hears all the little sounds because he doesn't sleep
well and he is often up and about when the rest of us are
dead abed. He sees the first buds in the spring, notices the
first rise of water, hears the first birds twittering and the
first squirrels chattering. Spring is a season he loves because
there is life. Autumn makes him sad. "It's the little sounds,"
he said once, "it's the little sounds going away I mind. Sometimes," he grinned shamefacedly, "I feel like crying."

I think of James Agee and how he couldn't bear the pain
of life either, the suffering and loneliness of people and the
courage of little things, and the dying of insects and grass
and the cold iron of winter and the ache of daytime and the
dark endlessness of night. Joe Spires knows more about the
endlessness of night than anybody I know. He only sleeps
an hour or two at a time. The war did that to him.

Sometimes when I have one of my own occasional white
nights I remember that Joe is probably awake too. I don't
want him to be awake. I wish he might be sleeping. But
I know he probably isn't and it's comforting, for nothing is

lonelier than three o'clock in the morning when the world is still and only you are moving about.

. . . and the people next up the road cannot care in the same way, not for any of it: for they are absorbed upon themselves: and the Negroes down beyond the spring have drawn their shutters tight, the lamplight pulses like wounded honey through the seams into the soft night, and there is laughter: but nobody else cares. All over the whole round earth and in the settlements, the towns, and the great iron stones of cities, people are drawn inward within their little shells of rooms . . . and none can care, beyond that room; and none can be cared for by anyone beyond that room.*

Life fragmented and broke James Agee's heart and I think it almost does that of Joe Spires. He would hoot me out of the hollow for saying so, but all the little things weigh too much on him.

It wasn't a very little thing that came to weigh on me next. Late in May, in the most beautiful month of the year, our house almost completed, doom spoke in a loud voice and the sound of his trumpet voice was like echoless iron in my ears.

* *Let Us Now Praise Famous Men.* James Agee and Walker Evans. Boston: Houghton Mifflin Company, 1960, p. 54.

Chapter 15
Hospital Windows Have Narrow Views

To LEARN exactly how dear life is, you have suddenly to be faced with the possibility there isn't much left of it for you. I know of no better purge, at least temporarily, for all pettiness and meanness, for all minor dissatisfactions, for all greed and ambition, than to be told, "It may be cancer."

The day I came home from my doctor's office with that weighing on me there was an ironing sprinkled down and waiting to be done. Of all household chores I detest most ironing. And of ironing, I detest most doing Mister G.'s suntan cotton work pants.

It was the end of May and the world was very lovely. Outside the sun was shining and the air was heavy with the smell of ten thousand roses in bloom. A cloud of yellow butterflies hovered over them. But I could not see or hear or smell anything beautiful at that moment. One word kept hammering and hammering and 'hammering away at me — cancer. And the smell of death was very strong.

It was so unexpected.

We both knew something was wrong, of course, and we had even anticipated the need for major surgery. But not this. Not ever this.

My doctor had sent me to Louisville to a specialist the week before where a series of examinations and tests had been made. The results were to be given to me this afternoon.

The *Adair County News* was having one of its perennial crises and with the house nearly finished, with Edgar and our good friend Joe in control, Mister G. was temporarily helping out. He had asked me to stop by the office and give him the news before driving back to the country. Neither of us expected anything worse than a vexing hospitalization just when we were completing the house, just when hardly an hour went by without need of my presence to make a decision. A thousand things needing me, personally, were confronting us. But it couldn't be helped, we told ourselves. We'd just have to delay things until I was on my feet again.

I was still in a state of shock when I went by the office. It took me several hours, in fact, to begin to *feel*. Todd Jeffries, our friend as well as our doctor, had had a difficult time telling me. He had found it so difficult, in fact, that he had thought briefly of sending me back to the specialist and having him break the news. Then he had told himself, "No. She's my patient. I'll, by God, do it myself."

I recall that his face was so twisted and wry as he talked to me that my immediate reaction, of all things, was to comfort *him!* To say, "Oh, come now, Todd, it's not all that bad."

And I was still in that bemused numb condition when I told Mister G. But his face went paper-white. He touched me briefly, quickly, then began pulling off his printer's apron. "I'll take you home."

Without any sense of histrionics at all, not meaning to show courage or valor, simply reacting to the pressure of press day, I said, "You can't. It's press day."

"To hell with press day!"

"No. I'm all right and I'll *be* all right. Help get the paper out." And I walked away without giving him any chance to go with me.

Once home, however, and alone, the reaction set in and the numbness and shock left. My instinct was to wander and think and agonize, but I knew it wouldn't do. I had to do something with the rest of the afternoon, something *hard* and tiring, something purposeful and above all something routine, something which tied me to my life.

Ironing may not have been the wisest choice but it was there waiting to be done, so I ironed. It was an unusually large ironing, probably stacked away for several weeks, and there was an unusual number of Mister G.'s work pants. Normally I flapped them about irritably and dabbled at them hurriedly, content to get most of the wrinkles out and some makeshift of a crease in. But that afternoon I ironed seven pairs of work pants meticulously and painstakingly, taking infinite care with them, as though this might be my last chance ever to give them loving attention, and as though I felt ashamed at having ever handled them neglectfully. My hands touched them with a new tenderness. And I prayed what may seem a very strange prayer.

I believe that one's whole life should be a prayer, that the way one lives must be prayer in action, and I don't much hold with running to the Lord in crisis. Energy and resolution and intelligence in meeting crises have always seemed to me the kind of praying he would most certainly like to hear and the kind that would do the most good. But while I surely meant to offer that prayer, too, I found myself saying aloud, once, "Just let me keep on ironing Mister G.'s work pants, please!"

It struck even me as a little ridiculous, for there was nothing I loathed more and I knew very well that if I was spared and allowed to go on ironing Mister G.'s work pants it wouldn't be any time till I would not consider it a privilege and I would be flapping them around in irritation again.

I could laugh about it. And that was the turning point, the moment of truth. And perhaps the prayer began to be answered with the laughter. For when Mister G. came home, early but with the paper dutifully out, he found me calm, all self-pity gone, not only resolute but bounced back to a good fighting stance. He needed to find me that way for he was stricken and exhausted.

I pulled him to the sofa beside me. "Look. We don't accept this thing. These first tests are not conclusive. They only indicate that further explorations must be made. Todd says no good diagnostician would make a diagnosis on these findings. But he thought we should know the indications, and that's all they are. We are not going to die a thousand deaths. We are not going to believe this thing until it is a final fact. We are going to believe these tests indicate something more serious than we thought, but we shan't say cancer or think cancer or act cancer until we know beyond any doubt it *is* cancer."

"You're not afraid?"

I told a bare-faced lie. "Nope."

I was, and I dare anybody to be told they may have cancer and not be scared out of their wits, but there wasn't any use two of us being witless. "Now this," I went on, "is what I want us to do. We are not going to alter any circumstance of our lives. We are going ahead with every plan we've made and neither of us is going to behave for a single instant as if we had any doubt, ever, that every plan is going to be carried out."

It was wonderful to watch Mister G.'s shoulders begin a slow brace back, watch his chin come up, and watch his eyes lose much of their troubled look. He grinned at me. Mister G. never deals in sentimentalities, but for once he nearly did. " 'I'm arm'd with more than complete steel,' " he quoted Shakespeare at me, " 'the justice of my quarrel.' "

"You're darned tootin'," I said irreverently and made us each a lovely, beautiful, marvelous, stout bourbon-and-branch-water highball.

We did as we had agreed. Mister G. kept right on helping at the *Adair County News* and Edgar, Joe and I, kept right on minding the store at the house. I couldn't help feeling pretty noble, though, until something right out of Don Quixote happened to me. I came down with the worst case of shingles ever seen just a week before I was to enter the hospital in Louisville.

Everybody laughs at shingles, I don't know why, for it's

no laughing matter. Something so painful you can't bear clothing to touch the inflamed skin, and so painful you might as well have toothache in your bones, is a little hard for me to grin over. Besides, there was the ridiculousness of it. I felt my nerves had betrayed me! *Some* windmills will tilt back at you, I found.

Medical men are divided in their opinions on the cause of shingles. Modern men incline toward the theory, and with some reason, that a virus similar to the one which causes chicken pox is responsible and they insist it is contagious. There was room to believe this, for Mister G. had had a light case of shingles not too long before, and while it was still in the future, Mister G.'s mother was to have it about six months after I did. It did look as if it was running through the family.

But more old-fashioned men cling to the belief it is caused primarily from nervous tension.

I wouldn't know, but it's no fun to have. And though nearly all doctors say it doesn't, I know one more thing about it. Once you've had it, it will recur again and again, traveling into the strangest places over your body. If it's caused by a virus it's the most persistent and long-lived little bug ever to exist.

Obviously I couldn't undergo surgery until the shingles abated so Todd pumped massive injections of something into me every other day for two weeks, then pronounced me, though I was still spotted and peeling and scaling, as ready as I was ever going to be.

Before surgery, my resolution to go through this entire business with a minimum of fuss, without getting into a flap, weakened at only one point. I did want my daughter with me. It meant calling her away from her husband and three sons but I found I was quite selfish enough to do it. I needed her gaiety and I knew it would not falter. Even though I was asking her to come and be frightened with me, and I was frightened, I knew that no amount of fear would keep her from providing me with the high jinks of the old days when we two stood alone but together against the world. I thought, too, she could bolster Mister G. a little.

Mister G. wanted more than Libby's frail feminine shoulder to lean on, however. He wanted Todd Jeffries! I never felt such a fool as when I had to ask Todd if he would come, if he would come and put on gown and mask and stand, just stand, in the operating room during that lengthy operation. "It's Mister G.," I said. "He thinks nothing can happen to me if you're there."

Todd laughed. "I'll be there."

In the event, he couldn't be. Another patient took a critical turn, lay lingering agonizingly so that Todd could not leave her, until she died just about the time I was taking my first wobbling steps after surgery. But the fact that without hesitation he had agreed served Mister G. almost as well. And of course we were in touch with him by telephone for I don't know how long.

Todd's best friend and roommate at medical school was my anesthesiologist and it was comforting in both the exploratory and the major surgery to have him sit beside me and tell me tales of their school days, and to find him still sitting beside me when I waked, ready to grin and tell me more.

"You do *not* have cancer!"

That was after the exploratory. Libby was in the room with me but Mister G. had gone out for a while and was not there to see Dr. Lyman Gray bend a quizzical look at me over the rims of his glasses as he announced the good news, or hear me give one hiccupy sob, or see Libby's fine dark eyes round and suddenly shine with tears.

In spite of what I had told Mister G., in spite of all my determination to be normal and casual about all this, I had been prepared for the worst verdict. I had, in fact, been expecting it. The prognosis, it seemed to me, just wasn't good enough. But the final say is always the pathologist's report. "Pre-cancerous lesions, yes — in another month, two months, six at the most . . . surgery is indicated. We'll operate at seven in the morning."

How good can God be to you! I know exactly how it feels to have a death sentence commuted. Mentally I had walked that last mile, but it was wonderful, wonderful to be able to retrace my steps.

We all went a little mad and we had a hilarious party in my room that night, Libby, Mister G. and some devoted friends. Dr. Gray allowed me a martini and dinner trays were brought up for the whole group. Even the floor nurse was indulgent about visiting hours. She just stuck her head in the door, put her finger on her lips to ask for a little less noise, closed the door and forgot us.

Surgery was a snap, now, and I breezed through it with a minimum of discomfort, with a high heart and a singing joy racing all through me. The nurses were endlessly kind, friends were in constant attendance, and my room was usually crowded and noisy with laughter. When Libby had to go home, Pansy came and stayed until the need for daily attention had passed.

Our good friend Joe Covington, coming for his first visit,

took one look when he entered, gasped, turned on his heel and went straight to his car for a bottle of Dowling's. He presented it to me solemnly. "Obviously," he said, "you're not sick. You've just found a new place to give parties."

He had found me sitting up in bed, like a queen on her throne, a corsage pinned to my bed jacket, nurses hovering, while a photographer from the *Courier-Journal* took pictures of my hefty lunch tray. All of us were in a convulsed state because of a news item about me in that morning's paper, concerning my affair with a canary-yellow hard-top Mercury convertible and its accompanying cartoon.

I drove a car when I was a girl but not for twenty years had I taken hold of a wheel, when suddenly I determined that kind of foolishness had to stop. Every other woman in the United States drove and I felt extremely silly when it was taken for granted I did too. Besides, it cost Mister G. a lot of time to drive me around to club meetings and speaking engagements and I thought his time too valuable to be spent chauffering me about.

I determined to buy my own car.

Mister G. viewed this with less than enthusiasm. It was his considered opinion that with my woolgathering habits I would be a menace to the general welfare if turned loose on the highway. I pooh-poohed this notion and hied myself to a used car lot owned by a friend of ours. I was cautious enough to decide on a used car, just in case. If I wrapped it around a utility pole there was no point making an accordion out of an expensive new car.

My demands were simple. I wanted a good car with automatic drive, for what beset me and confused me most was having to use two feet and two hands simultaneously. To me it was as awkward as rubbing your head and patting your stomach. Our friend had nothing on the lot at the time but he promised to keep me in mind.

A few days later he brought out for my inspection a three-year-old Mercury hard-top convertible. It was canary-yellow, not at all the discreet little number I had in mind, but he said it was a good, clean car and not too big for me. I had told him, also, I wanted a fairly small car because Henry's Buick made me feel as if I was steering the *Queen Mary* into dock.

The exhaust seemed rather noisy to me when he took me for a short drive and I mentioned it. He said the car had twin mufflers but that if it bothered me they could easily be removed and a single pipe installed. I didn't think it would bother me that much, especially when I learned I'd have to foot the bill. I convinced myself the color of the car didn't matter and I convinced myself I could put up with a muffled roar from the rear end so long as the engine was in good shape and wouldn't die on a hill, which all standard-gear cars have a vexing and obstinate way of doing with me. Even when I was a girl I used to drive miles around the slightest hill to keep from having to shift gears and suffer the inevitable dead engine and the frantic searching for brake, starter, clutch, emergency, and with horns honking at me to send me further witless.

Mister G. drove the car around and said, "Seems O.K. Seems a pretty good car."

For a year, then, I drove illegally all over the back roads of the county, carefully avoiding all towns. I had no intention of taking the test for my driver's license until I was in excellent practice. I grew accustomed to seeing the men of the county grin a little when I roared by, but I thought it was the flashy color of the car that amused them.

Finally, boned up on the written examination, and as ready as I would ever be to park parallel, I set off — praying I would pull it off all right, Mister G. riding manfully with me into Columbia for the big event. He left me with the state trooper and went away to the newspaper office.

The trooper had me test the brakes, the lights, the clutch, and so forth first. I might add that I had made certain the car was in apple-pie condition. Everything worked perfectly and smoothly. Eventually he asked me to start the motor. I did. He listened thoughtfully, then rather casually asked me to press the accelerator to the floor. Unfortunately he was standing too near the twin exhausts and as they roared and blasted I had the stomach-sinking experience of seeing his hat go cartwheeling across the street. Chasing it, he motioned for me to cut the motor off.

He returned grim-faced. "Lady, who owns this car?"

"I do."

I was fat and grandmotherly, with more than one gray hair in my head. His eyebrows lifted. "This is your *own* car?"

"It certainly is my own car. I bought it myself and it is registered in my own name."

Slowly he wiped his hand over his face. "I'm sorry, lady, but I can't give you a driving test today."

"Why not?"

"Your car has hot-rod mufflers on it. They're illegal."

Mortified beyond speech, I clambered out and looked at the offending double pipes. The trooper pulled his book out. "It's against the law to drive with hot-rod mufflers," he said.

I felt my face go hot. I wondered if he also thought I

drag-raced down by the bridge! I assured him I hadn't known they were hot-rod mufflers. He looked exasperated. "Couldn't you hear that roar?"

"Oh, I heard it all right," I said, "but I just thought all twin mufflers were noisy. Lots of cars have twin mufflers," I added hopefully and I pointed at his own. "Yours does."

"There's a difference," he said stiffly.

I was learning that for myself.

He never once cracked a smile. If he thought it was funny for a middle-aged woman to be driving a canary-yellow hard-top convertible with hot-rod mufflers he didn't act like it, and I didn't think it would be very funny if he learned that not only had I broken the law by driving a car with hot-rod mufflers, but I had been breaking it for a year by driving it without a license!

He twiddled his book and pondered while I stood and quaked. But I suppose I looked exactly like the foolish, naïve sort of woman who *would* do precisely what I had done. The very fact that I had innocently come to take a driving test in it practically proved my ignorance. Finally he put his book away. "O.K. lady, I won't give you a ticket this time, but you leave this car parked right where it is and have a garage come haul it away. Don't drive it another inch."

I vowed I wouldn't and I marched down to our friend's garage and raised merry hell with everybody connected with the business. Then I went to the newspaper office and raised merry hell with Mister G.

I still don't know whether our friend and Mister G. ganged up on me or not. I can't believe *both* of them failed to recognize hot-rod mufflers when they saw them. And they did take a longish drive together before I bought the car. And Mister G. did eventually write a very funny piece about the whole episode in his column, "Spout Springs Splashes." And the *Courier* did pick up the whole column and reprint it. But by that time I was too pleased to be recovering from surgery and my sense of humor had been restored and I could laugh as loudly as anybody that day Joe Covington called and thought a party was going on in my hospital room.

The *Courier* has not always courted me in hospital rooms, however.

I have not forgotten, nor am I ever likely to forget, our first attention from the Louisville *Courier-Journal*.

It meant so much to us when my first book was published to have it reviewed generously in their pages, and shortly afterward to have Mr. Cary Robertson, the Sunday editor, write and ask if we could come up to his office for an interview.

The Enduring Hills came out in April of 1950. We were living hand to mouth at that time on the little forty-acre place. No penny of royalties had yet been paid over and would not be until August. Mr. Robertson's letter actually caught us at a time when we were completely at the bottom of the barrel. Something was wrong with the fuel pump of our old car and we couldn't drive to Louisville. But we *had* to go. It meant too much to us to have a story in the Sunday *Courier*. So we must go by bus, which is still the only public transportation into and out of Adair County.

The rub here was that we didn't have bus fare. We sat down and did some figuring and came up with a minimum amount. Round-trip fares for two, plus I think it was two dollars we decided on for lunch. I thought about packing a sandwich lunch but was afraid there might be no place to eat it. But we certainly couldn't count on being taken out for the meal. Nobody was going to roll out the red carpet for us.

Mister G. put on his boots and began walking the hills hunting ginseng. He dug the roots and when there was enough of them, sold them to Leon Christie in Knifley. All our local stores used to buy "sang" roots, for digging "sang" has always been a quick way for our hill people to raise a few dollars in a crisis. The ginseng is passed on to a wholesale house in Louisville and from there I think the market is China where it is highly valued. For what I don't really know — either a medicine or an aphrodisiac.

Ten dollars in hand and our old clothes furbished up, we ventured to drive the old car to Campbellsville where we parked it and took the bus to the city. We arrived a little late, and worried because of it. Mr. Robertson had said eleven o'clock but the ways of buses cannot be foretold and we had dallied and coughed and struggled until we were twenty minutes behindhand. We made a dash for the *Courier* building one block down the street, arriving in a breathless rush.

We could have saved our breath. To say there was an anticlimax is putting it mildly. Not only had no one there ever heard of us, no one had heard of the appointment, and Mr. Robertson had not yet come in. We were an embarrassment of riches, but they were most kind to us. They sort of shuffled us around and tried to make us comfortable and they did their best to get hold of *somebody* who knew *something* about what was supposed to take place.

Mr. Robertson was reached finally and asked us to wait. Since that was what we were already doing it was a redundancy but we agreed. Then somebody suggested a staff photographer might take some pictures while we waited. That was a safe bet. If there was going to be a story, there must be pictures. Mr. James Keen, who has since become one of our favorite photographers on the *Courier*, likes to recall that it was he who harried us into a studio and took up about thirty minutes of the slack posing and shooting us.

It was quite obvious that Mr. Robertson had entirely forgotten the appointment. He is a dear person and we are now most fond of him, but I think he is a little absent-minded. It has nothing to do with the fact that he is one of the best Sunday editors in the country. One look at the Sunday *Courier* will confirm that. It just has to do with one of Mr. Robertson's personal quirks.

Not that he confessed he had forgotten us — not at all. He came in pretty breathless himself and there was much scurrying about. But eventually the truth could no longer be hidden. In his letter he had said Lois O'Neil, editor of the book page, would do the interview. Reached by telephone Lois O'Neil knew nothing about the proposed interview and her plans for the day were fixed and she could not alter them. Finally we were dumped into the unwelcoming lap of James Goble, a feature writer. He had never heard of the book, much less read it, and with his own work to do the Gileses were two people he could very well have done without. But bless him he was a good reporter with a good reporter's instincts. Halfway through the interview he threw his pencil down and said, "Look, this is a good story. It's too good a story to waste this way. You people go back home and I'll come down there and bring a photographer with me and we'll do a feature for the Magazine that will make their hair stand on end."

I didn't know whether he simply felt sorry for us, for by this time I was so humiliated and angry and so near the verge of tears because of all the hustling and bustling about and the obvious oversight when it had cost us so much in effort to make the trip at all that I was ready to walk out on the whole deal — or whether he really did feel there was a good story. And I didn't much care. I just wanted to go home.

Whatever the reason, though, James Goble was as good as his word. He and Tommy Miller, the photographer, did a feature on us that was warm and enthusiastic and generous beyond words. I showed a copy of it to Joe Creason, who usually does the *Courier* stories on us now, just the other day. It has become something of a museum piece but I keep it to remind me, when I become prideful, that we had a hard beginning and it's just as well never to forget it.

The *Courier* has been unfailingly good to us ever since. Long ago a new book of mine ceased getting a routine review. It gets special attention, usually the shrewd eye of Joe Creason who likes to combine his estimate of the book with something special about the author. Joe can throw you a light punch when he thinks you need it, but never a dirty one.

To interview us means he must spend a day with us, for we are a hundred miles from Louisville. It's a kind of running interview with the photographer taking pictures all over the place at unexpected times, and with Joe following me about, for although he may be a special feature writer he is also a man with a stomach and must be fed.

In the five or six hours of the loose, formless kind of thing we have all become accustomed to, and feeling as we do that Joe Creason is our good friend, and enjoying him as much as we do, we are very apt to say some things we would not say in a more formal setting. We have only to warn him it's off the record and we know it will *be* off the record. Not once has he ever violated our trust in him.

I think he likes our occasional explosions, our infrequent displays of temper about some prejudice or obliqueness, but he never uses them. He only gets a fuller flavor of our personalities which he more kindly reflects.

Being interviewed can be a treacherous thing, as we have learned. If the reporter happens to be in a foul mood for any reason, indigestion, a quarrel with his wife, or the ungodly hour you're arriving at an airport, he can make you look a fool and some take a sadistic pleasure in doing so. They see so many near-greats, so many poseurs, so many press-agented nobodies, they tend to look on everybody as a publicity hound, a headline seeker. If they're in that mood, if they're that cynical, the less you can say and the sooner you can get it over with, the better it is all around. We've been hurt very little by that kind of reporter.

But even the best-intentioned reporter can occasionally throw you a curve. I recall once making an off-the-cuff remark to a very sympathetic and understanding reporter. A new book was coming out. She — it was a woman — asked if we were going to New York for publication day.

It was one of those all-day interviews and we were in the kitchen where she was helping chop lettuce and radishes and celery for salad. In that folksy, cozy environment my guard was momentarily down. "Good Lord, no!" I said. "Why should we?"

She laughed. "Some writers like the glory. And it might help sell a few books."

Bluntly and unthinkingly, tucking a pan of rolls into the

oven, I replied, "We write books. We don't sell them."
Instantly I knew it was an indiscreet thing to have said.
"That," I warned, "is off the record."

"Sure," she laughed and I relaxed.

I don't think for one minute that she went straight to
Western Union and wired the journalist who then had a
column in the *New York Times* Book Review Section. I
think she simply saw him a few weeks later in New York and
in the course of conversation — perhaps even admiringly because she had made some caustic remarks about authors who
go dashing about the country autographing, lecturing, appear-
ing on television and at literary parties — repeated what I had
said. But if she had scruples about using the story, he had
none. It appeared in his column as a bald and arrogant and
insufferable statement: "We write books. Let the publisher
sell them." He predicted we had a short future.

I could only give thanks for the Houghton Mifflin attitude
toward their writers. In the eleven years they have been our
publishers not once has pressure been applied to stimulate us
to activity of any kind to publicize our books. With what is
now an almost old-fashioned reverence for writing and
writers, they leave you alone to do your job your own way.
They have never been guilty of even the most minor editorial
violation. They did not mention this remark, which they
could not possibly have missed, and thinking an explanation
would only make bad matters worse, we did not bring it up.
They will learn now, for the first time, what lay back of it
and of our great embarrassment.

Since that episode, of our own wish and desire we have
done some promotional work in television and autographing
parties. It has been in areas of the country with a special

interest in us and upon insistent invitation — invitations so insistent, in fact, that to refuse would have been ungracious and ungrateful. Houghton Mifflin have been unfailingly cooperative, unfailingly generous and helpful. I am in love with my publishers and make no bones about it. And someday, so help me, I am going to Boston and meet them. For, and this is probably as rare an oddity as ever existed in the publishing field, I have never visited my publishers and have only met, once and briefly, the editor-in-chief, Paul Brooks. That dear man, Oliver Swan, who is my agent with the Paul Reynolds firm, persuaded me to go to New York once. I was so scared I couldn't keep a bite of food down for the two days I made myself stay. Paul Brooks came on from Boston. Though they had promised not to, I was afraid they would *make* me make a speech somewhere, or appear on radio or television, or take me to some literary party. I loathed every second I was there and only relaxed when I set my foot back on Adair County land! But I've come a distance since then and someday we're going to pack the old fire-engine red station wagon and make that leisurely tour through New England I've dreamed of making, and Boston and Houghton Mifflin are going to be thoroughly explored.

But in 1958 the bouncy, gregarious, exuberant patient of Norton Infirmary's Female Surgical Ward came home bouncing to get back into action. She fell flat on her face with a violent recurrence of shingles which sent her back to the hospital for another week and brought her home at last sadly subdued and ready, now, to follow doctor's orders.

"Write," Dr. Gray had said. "Begin a new book as soon as you get home."

The long list of physical "don'ts" he had given me should

have told me why he advised me so. For months I must not do the work, nor engage in the activities that were daily routine for me. To sit idle would have driven me insane. He knew it. So he said, write.

But he did *not* know we had a house just a wee mite short of being ready to move into and that all the finishing details were so exciting and engrossing I couldn't turn my mind to a book. And he did not know, either, that a writer's work habits can become as rigid as poured concrete. Charles Dickens used to haul all the bits and pieces that cluttered his desk at home — his small green quartz frog, his special ink-well, his special pen wiper and holder — with him on his travels. He couldn't write a word until they were in place before him. Other writers have their peculiarities and habits and quirks. Mine has nothing to do with material things. It is the time of year I work. Having spent the biggest part of my life in an environment controlled by school terms I am most comfortable at work and work best if I begin a book in September and write through the winter finishing around June. Even when a book must go over the summer I usually lay it aside for the hottest months, for I simply do not write well during those months. A horse can travel with a burr under his saddle but he'll twitch and sidle and kick and be slowed and he won't cover the distance as well.

This was July. In every way it went against the grain to begin a book. But after my humbling and salutary lesson there was no alternative unless I wanted to sit with folded hands. I did it, but I did it with bad grace and gave Mister G. and my mother, who had come to hold the frayed edges of our household together, a pretty rough time of it. Incidentally, I had to throw out every word I wrote before

September, but at least for a few hours a day I was out of my family's hair.

I was glad when the whole business of illness and recovery was finished. I loathe being ill, not only for the usual reasons of discomfort and inconvenience but because it affronts one's sense of dignity. Laughter and tears and human dignity are the most important differences between man and other living creatures. Illness, and especially surgery, violates human dignity more than anything I know. The things that are done in the name of medicine are shattering, and while one is grateful for the skill and knowledge, it remains true that all sense of individual human dignity is gone and what is left is but a poorly functioning piece of machinery.

I reached the depths of this realization one morning in the hospital as I wrote my daughter that the most important thing in my world was whether my "suspended" and stitched-up bladder would function properly and daily. "The windows," I wrote, "of a hospital room are very narrow and the view is very restricted."

Bladders! What an intellectual horizon!

I'm not sure Mister G.'s old uncle isn't right. To go under the knife, he says, is to die. Death has dignity. But what can you say for bladders?

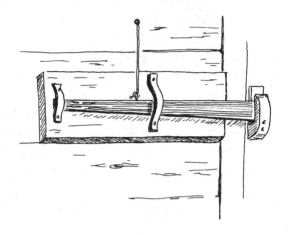

Chapter 16
A Heap of Living

IT HAS BEEN a rainbowed house, sun-blessed for the most part but occasionally rain-drenched as all good houses ought to be. It is beautiful and mellow and kind and loving. At the same time it's cranky sometimes as all old things are. It has its stubborn streaks, its inflexible will and its ancient pride. It's as if occasionally it looked over its specs at us and warns, "Now you look here, young'uns, I've been around a long, long time. Don't try any tricks on me."

We have, but they haven't succeeded.

We tried to warm it the first winter without proper insulation or heating. It promptly sent every B.T.U. of heat right out through our lovely shingleboard roof and gloomed icily at us. I could swear the logs beetled their brows at me and drew apart in frozen and injured pride. A thousand tiny cracks and crannies opened up in them and the wind whistled through. We bought miles of a tubed calking and squirted it recklessly. It didn't behave as advertised and we searched in vain for a guarantee. The calking froze and cracked too. "It's no use," Mister G. said tiredly, "the answer is insulation."

I thought it would have helped to add more chinking but I couldn't persuade him.

We tried to fool the house into protecting the plumbing pipes by hiding them behind cupboards and inside boxing and walls. It belched them back at us in split sections the first time the thermometer dropped to twenty degrees. It didn't relent until at the end of two years I finally relented and allowed Mister G. to bring the pipes out into the open frankly and candidly. Then the house relaxed with a smile and placed never another obstacle to instant running water in any temperature.

We thought to ease our mountainous gas bills the second winter by supplementing with wood fires. Mister G. built a flue in the kitchen and ran an opening between logs into the dining room which we turned into a winter sitting room. He lined the opening with asbestos which I ignorantly believed to be heatproof. Less than joyously but from necessity we installed two gargantuan woodburning heaters, one in the kitchen, one in the dining-sitting room. We continued to use the small gas heater in the bathroom and we just closed off the two big rooms at the front of the house.

On a black, black January day when the pipes had been frozen for three days and I was washing dishes in creek water — the only water still running — I thought I smelled smoke. I sniffed again, decided it was the residue left from throwing another chunk on the fire, and kept on with my chore. Soon, however, smoke began to swirl about my head and I swiveled about. I was horrified to see the sitting room thick and foggy with boiling blue plumes. Fire! For a moment I was immobilized with terror. Fire, the greatest foe of country people, fire, before whose licking tongues a country house is helpless and doomed, fire was threatening my beautiful log house!

Mister G. was not at home. In the winter, as with all the other men of the community, he makes a daily sashay to the country store to catch up on news, prognosticate about the weather, play a game or two of checkers, loaf and whittle an hour or two. It's a countryman's coffee break. But at that moment I bitterly resented it. It seemed to me that in every crisis of my life since the day we were married Mister G. had not been where I needed him. He was always away, up the hollow, on the ridge, at the river, or at the store, when his man's strength was needed. There was no time to give it more than a fleeting thought. That could wait until this emergency was dealt with and then it would deserve something more than fleeting.

I dashed into the sitting room, fighting the smoke and choking on it. It was curling and boiling all about the stovepipe, and the pipe itself, in the flue hole, was red-hot. From cracks in the logs on either side smoke was pluming out too. But there were no flames. Smoldering, I thought. Ready instantly to burst into flames but still, thank God, just smoldering.

There was a bucket of creek water at the kitchen sink. I grabbed it and sloshed it over the stovepipe, fled to the creek for another bucket and sloshed again. I don't know how often I repeated it but it was enough to drown the floor, all the furniture, the curtains and walls. My wet houseshoes slowed me so I kicked them off and ran barefoot back and forth. Ordinarily the gravel near the creek would have made me mince wincingly. I didn't even feel it. I was too frightened and too concentrated on more and more water.

When no more smoke was boiling around the pipe I had only one thought. To yank the pipe out of the flue hole and make certain the fire was out by pouring more water down the hole. I didn't once think about a winter's collection of soot in the pipe. I gave a strong yank and was promptly buried in soot. It poured over me, onto the drowned floor, onto the soused furniture and curtains and all over the sweet, creamy-white wall. There was never a bigger mess. And there was never a blacker chimney sweep than I. I just shook myself and went on pouring water. I thought of that ancient round we sang when I was a child — "Scotland's burning, Scotland's burning, put it out, put it out, Fire, fire, fire, fire, pour on water, pour on water." It wasn't Scotland burning but something dearer to me and I certainly poured on water. I probably poured forty gallons too much but I wasn't taking any chances. And when I finished there was not the least bit of doubt the fire was out.

Normally when such a crisis is over I get the shakes and go weak-kneed and begin to cry. But for some reason, probably because Mister G. hadn't been there and indignantly I thought he should have been, I was angered into additional strength. I mopped and cleaned and scoured and scrubbed and threw away and threw out until no sign of the fire was left except the sodden hole in the flue.

Then, still furious, my anger turned on the frozen water pipes. Mister G. had given up on them. He had ripped away the baseboards and had tried a welding torch, electric heaters turned on full blast, hot water poured over them, everything he could think of. In disgust, finally, he had said, "They'll just have to thaw out when they're ready."

They jolly well wouldn't, I determined, they'd thaw out when *I* was ready. I marched into the bedroom, stripped our two electric blankets from the beds, and wrapped them cozily around the jelled but fully exposed pipes. I turned the thermostat on High and went back to finish the dishes.

When Mister G. came home from his checker game he had a charred log to chip out, a flue hole to mend, but there was hot and cold running water and for some unbelievable reason, no burst pipes this time. That gentle heat from the blankets must have done the loving kind of thawing the pipes needed.

When Mister G. came home my anger had blown itself out, too, and he was greeted only with the news he'd better get busy mending the flue hole before the pipes froze again. We couldn't, I said, keep them wrapped in electric blankets the rest of the winter.

But this was all hidden in the future that day of slow fire and steam, the nineteenth of August, 1958, when William Payne collected our chattels from the three separate roofs we had distributed them under, and moved us back to the banks of Spout Springs Branch. Once more he brought his big truck and most of his relatives and heaved and hove and shoved and pushed all our unwieldy effects about.

My mother was calm and managing and the move was achieved with a minimum of bother for me. Indeed I might have been four again. *"Don't* lift that chair!" "You've been on your feet for an hour. Sit *down!"* Four weeks out of the hospital I was still hedged around with don'ts. In heaven to be at the helm of a family again, needed, supervising, giving orders, directing, she banished me finally to the new house. "And be sure you *sit* while you tell them where to place things."

There is nothing like moving into a brand-new house even if it's built of old logs. It's so clean, so specklessly, spotlessly clean. And it smells so good. And there is, for a few days at least, so much room for everything, so much space, so little clutter. The floors gleamed with wax and the men obediently brought in things as I directed . . . rugs first, then furniture, each piece set where it belonged, beds put up as they were brought in, boxes here, there, and beyond, labeled and packed for the rooms they belonged in. It was an orderly, masterful move and highly gratifying.

It should have been, and almost was, a time of unalloyed joy for me. It was the house of my dreams built to order for me. But I was tense and full of emotion and still more ill than I knew. And when it was done, everything miraculously neat and put away, there came for me an inevitable moment.

I have been as peripatetic a human being as ever lived. I have moved probably forty or fifty times in my restless shifting about and always, no matter how much I have bettered my condition, no matter how much I have looked forward to the move, no matter how practical and sane I know it is, there comes that moment when strange walls stare at me and refuse to have me. Like a homeless child I long for something and know no more than a child what it is I want. I only know, until my commonsense says nonsense to me, I want none of this.

It came for me now as the sun set and the long summer twilight crept in. The logs glowered and gloomed, the rooms were too big, the ceilings were too high, and the creek outside was too noisy. Why had I thought I wanted it?

With my practical mind I knew it was nerves and letdown. It was always that. So long as I could keep busy, so long as there was the struggle to achieve, so long as there was the goal ahead, I was happy. The end reached, always, there came this moment of strangeness, this feeling of being lost. I have it each time a book is finished, also. I struggle and labor for nine months or a year on each one, coming to loathe the book and hate the struggle, yet feeling only a day's relief when the end has come and nothing but uneasiness until I can begin another.

I went into the big bedroom which, because we hadn't been able to finish it as I had wished, seemed like the anteroom of a barn to me and cried a little, and that was that. There was a meal to be cooked, the first supper in our new home, and it must be a celebration. No snacks tonight. Thank God for the body's needs, I thought, thank God for the daily routine. And I went to open a bottle of white wine.

Here in the valley the days may be very hot but the nights are nearly always cool, especially in August. As the dark deepened that evening the chill crept down the hollow and lay over the creek. We shivered and said, a fire. We must build our first fire on the hearth. There was no proper firewood yet but there was no lack of discarded rafters and posts, boarding and shingles. We scavenged them up and piled them near the door. Mister G. laid the fire and I handed him a match. His hand hesitated one single small second before he touched it to the crumpled newspaper which would set the kindling aflame and his eyes flicked at me. But that was what the lost child was looking for. That one brief glance which said I belonged someplace, belonged to *somebody*. This *was* home. This *was* what we had wanted and built and it *would* cherish and protect us.

A great peace settled over me and as the flames licked up the dry wood and it began to crackle and spark, as the smoke drew beautifully straight up Mister G.'s perfectly built chimney, I knew that nothing ever again would really threaten that inner peace. Whatever storms came, and I knew they would come, Mister G. and I had a home, of the spirit as well as of the body.

We sat for a long time before the fire, the coffeepot on the hob to keep it warm, and we talked and talked and talked. Then we made a loving tour of the whole house. We knew we had built well. The logs had been sealed on the interior against woodborers and wasp eggs with gym floor sealer. It had darkened them a little but given them gloss. The firelight danced over them and flickered back into our eyes. Overhead in the living room were the two- by eight-inch beams, a little blackened from other fires, nail studded here and there, but strong and beautiful.

The paint in my study — temporarily my mother's bedroom — and the dining room and hall was pure and softly creamy. The bathroom gleamed with chrome and porcelain and we grinned as the toilet gushed a spring of sparkling water at a touch. No more necessaries on icy mornings. I forgot I had wanted apricot fixtures and brass fittings. I just gave thanks for the cheapest white and the efficient chrome.

The kitchen was the priceless room to me, the heart of the house. Overhead were the square beams Mister G.'s great-great-uncle had hewed, his ax marks still showing. Along two walls ran the satiny-doored cupboards Mister G. had made of the mellow old poplar boarding in the same ancestral uncle's little frame house. Every door had been planed by Mister G. and sanded and sanded, then lovingly waxed. He had made the cupboard posts of chestnut and brass hinges held the doors in place. He had battened the doors with maple bars and the pulls were whittled, long slim bars of blue poplar against the golden yellow of the doors.

Under the windows, which looked onto the creek (and already the bird feeder) was the great square oak table we loved. And against a divider, one side of which lined up the cooking range and a cooking counter, sat the shabby old faded red sofa. Near it was Mister G.'s big chair. It was a happy room, I thought, a good room, a pleasant and cheerful room. I said so and Mister G. nodded and agreed. "It's going to be a good house." So we slept our first night under our hand-rived shingleboards, and we slept well.

It is now almost five years since that night and though it has had its crankinesses the house has been all we hoped it would be. Each year we have done a little more finishing, but not until 1961 could we afford the expensive job of insulating properly and installing a good heating system. *Johnny Osage* did that for us. We let out our belts a little when we saw the size of the first royalty check and Mister G. promptly put eight inches of rock wool between us and the shingleboards and drifted it down the walls of the nonlog middle section.

To make sure we then added what in some opinions is an anachronism for a log house. We had storm doors and windows installed. We preferred, we told all scoffers, to be warm. Let somebody else be purist. And we were blessedly warm that winter, all over the whole big house, with no wood fires to tend, save the one in the fireplace and that only when we wanted it. The heating bill was reduced at long last to a sensible amount. It took me an entire winter to grow accustomed to having the whole house at my disposal. For three winters we had shut off the big living room and bedroom and moved into the dining-sitting room and converted my study into a bedroom. I wandered blissfully about soaking up the good heat, feeling as free as a bird with so much room again. Though Mister G. continued to use his electric blanket on occasion, mine became a thing of the past. Wonders, I thought, would never cease.

There are two more projects before we can call the house finished, if a house is ever actually finished. The big bedroom remains barny and must be ceiled and paneled and wall-carpeted. Don't ask me why. I just have a need for a bedroom to be a little elegant. And we want wide screened porches running across the front and the whole length of the house. We want doors opening onto the wide porches from every room. In summer we like a house to be outdoors as nearly as possible. Occasionally I wonder which book will give us the finished bedroom and which will give us the porches. It would be a neat coincidence if this one could do its part.

In five years we look back on much happiness and many joyous times. The logs have heard a lot of laughter, a lot of good talk, a lot of fine music, few harsh words and almost no weeping.

Our first Thanksgiving at Spout Springs was most genuinely a day of giving thanks. It was the first time we gathered under our roof the "coterie," the "gang," the blessed hedonists. Joe Covington came bearing Dowling's and we christened the huge heavy double front door with a proper libation.

The door has no lock. For several years Mister G. contrived a lock of sorts from a tenpenny nail, but my mother eventually had made for us a latch, a bar of walnut wood which raises and lowers with a rawhide thong. In the daytime the thong is shoved through a tiny hole in the door. This custom gave rise to the old saying the latchstring is out. At night we pull it in. But we saved the tenpenny nail. Our friends mean to have it gilded for us.

Joe, who was trifling with the affections of a girl in South Carolina at the time, had driven all night and most of the day to reach us for dinner that Thanksgiving. We chided him. "I would," he insisted, "have mushed by dogsled through a blizzard to be here."

Ruth's dinner was superb.

Ruth White became a part of our house on the day we moved into it. Since then she has provided an extra pair of hands, a cheerful countenance, a willing heart, regularly. She has helped polish and shine the house, has washed and ironed our clothing, and in that first difficult year after surgery when occasionally I did not feel entirely well, often lifted my spirits with her consistent good humor and happiness.

When there is a "getherin'" she comes to help with the dinner and to "redd up" afterward. I think she enjoys our getherings very much and our friends are all attached to her.

That Thanksgiving Ruth arrived in her clean white uniform, her nice chocolate-brown face shining happily. But what we felt was especially endearing, what all of us loved and will never forget in her thoughtfulness, was her new apron. Stenciled across its front were the words: Welcome to our house!

It made our own welcome warmer.

Each year the colored people of our community have a revival which, since time began, has been called the "August meeting." Mister G. attended it as a boy and so far as I know his father also attended. It is looked forward to by the whole community and everybody goes. When I went, my first time, I saw a different Ruth than I was familiar with in my home.

The music was quite literally "out of this world." Rejoice, they shouted, and make a joyful noise unto the Lord, and they did truly rejoice and make joyful noises for a full hour before the "preaching" began. Besides the glorious voices there were a piano, guitar, tambourine, drum, and brass cymbals. It was Ruth who handled the cymbals with deftness and an intricate rhythm, her small body swaying, her head thrown back as she raised her voice in song.

When the singing closed finally it was with a beautiful song:

> Anybody asks you who I am,
> Who I am,
> Who I am,
> Anybody asks you who I am,
> Tell him I'm a child of God.

Whatever else Ruth White is, neighbor, friend, helper in the home, above all, and first, she is radiantly a child of God. I understood better her glowing warmth in our home.

The music was good that night. Mister G.'s guitar was inspired and Pansy taught us a new song — That Picture of My Mother on the Wall. We caterwauled it to our heat-leaking roof, piled logs on the fire, brewed more gallons of coffee, and felt god-blessed.

The first Christmas we had Pansy and Russell again, and

Russell's brother Owen and his pretty wife, Alma. I have no family east of the Mississippi. I am a westerner by birth and all my people live west. Pansy and Russell have no family left except his brother and his spinster sister who lives in Texas. We put up barriers against Christmas loneliness and Christmas nostalgia for childhood's stockings hung by the fire together — and it was good, though it did not quite accomplish what it was meant to accomplish. But the old house held us and was kind.

In the summer the grandsons came and we had them for two long golden months. We made blackberry jam, sixty pints of it, and peach preserves, and they ate until they rounded with fatness of fried chicken, corn on the cob, green beans, great red tomatoes from the garden, and always and always hot biscuits and cream gravy. From their favoritest grandfather they had caught the habit.

They fished and swam, went on picnics, built a tree house, painted the old skiff and rowed it up and down the creek, grew freckled or brown according to their skins, had their usual poison ivy, mashed the usual number of fingers, stumped the usual number of toes.

My nephew, John Holt III, was married in New London, Connecticut, that June. His bride jet-flew from San Diego for the wedding but, finishing submarine school the day before he was married, Johnny meant to motor her on a month-long honeymoon back across the country. Two years before he had been graduated from Annapolis and the Navy was his career. His new station was San Diego again. Thriftily Johnny planned to visit all across the country. It would introduce his new wife to his relatives and it would also save money.

Our boys were excited to nervous fidgets over the forthcoming overnight visit from the bride and groom. Bart painted a welcome sign to hang on the door. He took his idea from an anniversary plate Buddy Lowe had had Pansy paint for our tenth wedding anniversary. Two lovebirds perch on a limb, billing and cooing over a Victorian Henry and Janice. Bart couldn't accomplish Johnny and Valerie and he settled for blood-red cardinals on a twig and the Spanish "Bien venido" twined on a pale blue banner.

They were to arrive in the late afternoon. A festive dinner was arranged. Aflutter the boys set the table lovingly. Then they bathed, dressed, and loafed nervously. "Why don't they come? Why don't they come?"

But Scott was most apprehensive about another matter. Breakfast in Kentucky meant ham or fried chicken or an entire pound of bacon or sausages, with scads of eggs and hot biscuits and gravy, *and* in July, *hot* blackberry jam. "Suppose," Scott wondered aloud, "just suppose she doesn't *like* a big breakfast. Some girls don't. Just suppose she's a toast-and-coffee girl?"

"We'll give her toast and coffee, then," I said, "and we'll simply eat our own big breakfast as usual."

The other boys were listening and they chimed in. "Yeah, Scott, that's the way to play it. Cool, man."

But Scott wasn't happy yet. "I shan't like her very much if she doesn't."

I had lost the thread a little. "Doesn't what, dear?"

"Doesn't like hot blackberry jam!" he wailed.

Light dawned. Scott had offered to pick the blackberries the next morning for of course *hot* blackberry jam must be made from fresh berries, not a minute more than fifteen from vine to kettle.

Mister G., as usual, came to the rescue. "Wanta bet?

I'll bet you a king-sized coke Johnny Holt wouldn't marry a girl that didn't like hot blackberry jam."

Scotty grinned and relaxed. He was very fond of his big cousin, Johnny Holt, and he hadn't thought of that angle.

They came, were appropriately welcomed, made the expected fuss over Bart's sign and asked sweetly if they might have it to keep forever. He was their willing slave after that. They ate, seemed glad of a quiet evening, and were eventually escorted to their room by Bart who was bursting with the knowledge that beds had been shifted about to give them a double bed. I couldn't quite face giving newlyweds the twin beds in our own room. Bart pointed to the bed and yelled, "Surprise!"

They thought he meant the gift which I had laid, for lack of any other place, on the bed. "Naw," he said frankly, "the bed, the bed. It's double."

It was indeed. I'm not sure they thought him as innocent as I knew he was.

We let them sleep a little late the next morning but the activity of the boys, in almost agonizing suspense now about Valerie's fitness to be a member of the clan, waked them eventually and, I suspect, still earlier than they would have liked.

Three little boys hurried to seat Valerie at the table when she emerged. Three pairs of young eyes, two blue and one deep brown, were lit with eagerness, anxiety, and nervousness, almost sick with hope that she would measure up, for they already liked her so much. She must have thought it odd, how fixed their gazes were.

Scott had picked roses for the table and the sun glinted through the windows onto shining silver, steaming coffee, hot biscuits wrapped in their napkin in a wicker basket, ham, red and odorous on a blue platter, flanked by scrambled eggs, and, *pièce de résistance*, in the place of honor right by Valerie's plate, the pot of *hot* blackberry jam.

The moment had come. The curtain was up. Would she or wouldn't she? The boys were on the edge of their chairs as food was passed and repassed. I felt like nudging Valerie and whispering, eat, girl, eat. Whether you like breakfast or not, this is tremendously important.

There need have been no worry. Valerie took generous helpings of everything that came her way, then manfully she ate her way through seconds. The boys relaxed, grinning. Valerie had as hefty a breakfast appetite as her young husband or any of her new young cousins. The climax came when she took more and more and more of the hot blackberry jam! Scott rolled his eyes at me in ecstasy, and I *had* to tell.

"And *you* picked the berries this morning?" she asked, laughing.

"Practically at daybreak," he assured her.

It was moving when I glanced at my young nephew to see his eyes misted. "I think that's the sweetest thing I ever heard," he said, over a catch in his throat.

Scotty nodded. "But you see," he said earnestly, "you just haven't *lived* unless you've had hot blackberry jam for breakfast."

Solemnly the bride and groom agreed that not even the nectar of the gods could give life more savor, and sealed themselves forever in our hearts.

And there was the family Christmas at Spout Springs one year, the biggest and the best. My brother, faced with his first loneliness at that season, his son and eldest daughter married and living far away, suggested the family come to our house. We leaped at the suggestion. "Come," we said, "all of you. The house will give at the seams."

And they came — my sister Mary and her husband Claud; my brother John and his wife Evelyn and the fifteen-year-old daughter, Penni; and our mother, Lucy McGraw Holt. My sister came five days early because, faithful Martha that she is, she wasn't about to allow me the work of preparation alone. We baked and roasted and stewed and thawed frozen water pipes and did last-minute shopping, bought glitter for our hair and made hot rum punch to greet the late arrivals on Christmas Eve. John and Evelyn, Penni and Lucy McGraw couldn't leave till the last minute because of Penni's social calendar.

But they did come, lights gleaming in the snowy dusk, horn blaring, heads stuck from windows, screams and shouts and hugs and joy to the world! We all got a little tipsy, on love as much as rum punch and over supper, in his glee, my sister's husband got his tongue tangled. He waved his thrice-emptied cup and shouted, wanting music, "Deck the balls with house of folly!"

We decked them properly. We are a singing family and the old upright piano had just been tuned. My mother plays and so do I. We spelled each other. My sister is a lyric soprano and my brother has the sweetest tenor, outside of my father's, I have ever heard. My mother is an alto and I usually growl along with her. Mister G. is bass and Claud was baritone. Evelyn has a nice medium soprano and Penni just looked on. I think she thought we were all out of our minds!

I am prejudiced, of course, but I truly doubt many families sing as well together and that night, rich with being together again at Christmas for the first time in twenty-three years, we almost outdid ourselves. We came finally to tears for the missed father, gone from us for twenty years. The last time we had Christmas together his voice had led us.

Buddy Lowe and Pansy and Russell joined us on Christmas night and again there was music. It didn't stop in fact until three in the morning. Penni, who had been sulky about coming and missing her high school festivities, warmed and glowed under the spell of family and friends and music, and had what in her teen-age vocabulary she called "a blast." She who had been the most reluctant to come was in the end the most reluctant to leave, pleading at week's end for just one more day.

It was a week that did turn this old house into what it so badly wants to be, a roof over a big sprawling family. There were beds all over and people underfoot in every room, the buffet always groaning with food, friends coming and going at all hours, snacking and toasting what they were pleased to call the fabulous Holts. And the dear sister, the Martha-Mary, always replenishing, rinsing glasses, filling cups, slicing, serving, pouring, beating, baking. We would never have eaten a proper meal without her. I was too bemused.

When it ended and they drove away I felt left behind and forlorn. My needle pointed almost irresistibly west too. I had had a lot of the west that year, a lot of my family. A little resentfully I wondered why I should have to live in Kentucky. Deliberately I stripped the house of every sign of Christmas and railed at Mister G. about my exile. Quietly he answered me. "We will live anywhere in the world you want to live. Just say what you want."

It stopped me. Meekly I conceded that where I wanted

to live, really, was right here, on Spout Springs Branch. You can't have Christmas every day in the week. Tuck it away, I told myself. It's one more lovely memory. And get on with the job. The job was the next book.

Chapter 17

Is This Dam so Damn Necessary?

AT FIRST we didn't believe it.

"It's just another rumor," we said. "You know how these stories about the dam float around. We've been hearing them for ten years. Every day there's a new rumor and nothing has come of them yet."

"I, for one," I added stoutly, "don't believe any of these stories. I don't believe there is ever going to be a dam on Green River."

Our friend squinted at me through his cigarette smoke. He said quietly, "You know enough about politics to know that when somebody in Washington decides to build a dam, on any river, anywhere in the United States, it's as good as built. Somebody in Washington has decided there is going to be a dam on upper Green River. However long it's delayed, that dam is going to be built."

Unconvinced but shaken I stared at him. "You believe that, don't you?"

He nodded. "I believe it. The dam may not be built for five years but it's going to be built as sure as shooting."

We were troubled when he left but not personally troubled. We thought it a pity the river must be tampered with. Green River is a lovely stream, one of the most beautiful in the world, we think, and it grieved us to know it must be changed in any way, however far downstream from us. It rises in Lincoln County, less than sixty miles from us as the crow flies, and it flows generally westward across the state to its confluence with the Ohio in Daviess County. In its lower stretches it is a stately, deep river which we barely recognize. But here near its source it is as frisky and frolicsome as a happy child, nearly always shallow, with clear green water rushing over a white-pebbled floor. Along our particular three-mile piece it isn't even a river of moods. Rarely does it grow angry enough to pose much of a threat to bottomlands. Normally it is benign, beautiful and cleansing. Mister G. learned to swim in it and I suppose his father and his grandfather and his great-grandfather and all his uncles and his cousins by the dozens learned to swim in it. All his life Mister G. has fished this river and along this particular piece which flows through our valley I doubt if there is a riffle or a hole he doesn't know by repeated footfall in every season of the year.

We pondered at length this fairly new urgency of the federal government's to build dams on all watercourses and the anxiety of congressmen from all states to get for their own states as much appropriation as possible for water resources. Some of it, we knew, was badly needed. But some of it we strongly suspected smelled highly of the pork barrel. We couldn't tell about this dam. Maybe it was needed. Maybe lower down the river does do a great deal of flood damage. Maybe in the general interests of conservation it was best to stop that eternal washing away of the topsoil. At any rate there was nothing we could do about it. As our friend had said, when it is officially decided a dam is going to be built, it usually gets built and you may as well accept it.

But we could, and did, give fervent thanks it would not affect our particular piece of river. That, at least, would be left unchanged. Because everybody knew, it had been common talk for years, that the dam was to be located, if and when it was ever built, a few miles above the small town of Greensburg. This was thirty-five miles from us, sixty by river. Since it would be a small dam, creating a small lake, no longer than thirty miles at most, in no way could we be affected. It would not back the river up anywhere near us. The bulk of the lake, everybody said, would lie across Green and Taylor counties. This was of great comfort to us.

Time passed. Another year, perhaps.

And then, uneasily, we began to see engineers on our particular stretch of the river. "Oh, they're surveying the whole river," it was said, "doesn't mean a thing."

The engineers themselves were discreetly silent. They

admitted, for it couldn't be hidden, to making a survey but for what, and why, they never said. One joker at the local store quacked, "They've just got to use up all the money appropriated for the survey."

We saw them about for several months and then they finished their work and left. It was good not to see them around. I think we all felt relieved when they were gone. And nothing more was heard for quite a long time.

In October of 1961, when Mister G. and I were finally and at long last finishing the home we had been living in unfinished for three years, the first dam news we had heard since spring broke upon us. We already knew, from the Louisville *Courier-Journal*, that all preliminary work had been completed, the survey finished, and a dam location recommended. For some reason however the news item didn't mention the location.

Rumors began to fly thick and fast now. "They decided to build down at Greensburg," a neighbor told us.

"How do you know? Are you sure?" I had a paintbrush in my hand and Mister G. had a hammer in his. We stopped all work to listen.

"Fellow over there was up at the Engineers' office in Louisville. Said they told him. Everybody over at Greensburg's talking about it."

"If that's true," I sighed, "what good news it is!"

But we had learned to take all rumors with a grain of salt, even when a fellow had talked to a fellow that knew a fellow that had got it straight from the horse's mouth at the Engineers' office in Louisville.

The next day we heard a completely different story. Mister G. came home from the store quoting a still more reliable source. "Johnny Black said there wasn't any truth in that story going around yesterday. He said they found the rock formations near Greensburg too soft and full of potholes. They won't hold a dam."

"Where did he hear it?"

"Well, he talked to one of the surveyors."

"Where are they going to build it, then?"

Mister G. shook his head. "Fellow didn't say. Johnny thinks just above Lemmon's Bend."

I thought about that location. The river makes a great, looping bend just there, reinforced by high bluffs on one side but with nothing but a wide, stretching valley on the other. "I don't believe that," I said flatly. "There's nothing to tie to on the other side."

"Doesn't make sense to me, either," Mister G. admitted.

But Lemmon's Bend, if it did prove to be the location, was still in Green County, pretty far from us. It was nearer than Greensburg, true, but not too much.

I was beginning, however, to carry around with me mental pictures of the river below us. There was one place where it flowed for miles through a deep chasm. And Robinson Creek, one of the longest tributaries, which poured tons of flood water into the Green at every heavy rain, emptied into it just above that chasm. The mouth of Robinson Creek was also above the new, dreadfully expensive bridge the highway department had built only two years before. It didn't make sense to me they would have built it only to condemn it a couple of years later. That bridge had been bothering me a long time. A dam just below the mouth of Robinson Creek could tie on both sides to those steep, rocky bluffs and the bridge would also be saved. But dear

Lord, a dam just there would mean a lake backing up very, very close to us. Uncomfortably close.

Shortly afterward we heard the disquieting rumors that Robinson Creek *had* been chosen and recommended. Mister G. had a dull look in his eyes when he repeated it to me. Alarmed myself, my immediate thought was to comfort him. He looked so strangely vulnerable and youngly hurt. "It may not be so. We've heard a thousand rumors before. And even if the dam *is* built there, it's to be a very small lake. It *can't* reach us. There's nothing for us to worry about."

At such times your reaction is wholly personal. When a dam is built, somebody, somewhere, is going to be condemned and drowned and flooded out by the resulting lake, but it's always, please God, not you! Somebody's heart has got to ache. Somebody has got to walk the last time over land he knows the way he knows his own face in the mirror, has plowed and planted all his life and which perhaps his father and his grandfather before him plowed and planted. Somebody has got to pile his furnishings in a wagon or truck and drive away from walls and a roof that have sheltered him all his life, perhaps his family for generations. Somebody has got to start his life all over again, with money in his hand of course which the government has paid him, but in a strange community among strange neighbors. You know those things and they make you wince, but you still pray it won't be you. It's human and it's natural to want that cup to pass you by. And our house meant so much to us. We had put so much of ourselves into it, so much blood, sweat and tears. This just could not be its fate.

We didn't talk much about it. We couldn't. Like ostriches we just sort of buried our heads in the sand and hoped we wouldn't be seen.

It was during the Christmas holidays, and what a grim gift it was, that our friend brought us the authentic U.S. Corps of Engineers contour and elevation map of the dam and lake. He didn't say anything. He only unrolled the map on the dining table, weighted its four corners with the sugar-bowl, salt and pepper shakers, and a jar of mayonnaise. Small, irrelevant things like that have a way of engraving themselves forever on your memory. I may forget that map in time but I will never forget those four small articles which held it down so we could see.

Our eyes flew instantly to our valley and particularly to Spout Springs Branch, our own home. Water. Nothing but water. Over all of it. From the hills on the far side of the river to the hills on this side, and a long arm reaching up Spout Springs Branch which flows through our yard. That long arm filled our hollow from hill to hill and reached a considerable distance up its length.

Our friend's finger traced that arm of water so slowly and painfully and silently that a strange thing happened as I watched it. Suddenly the map changed and I was not looking at marks on paper. I was looking down into the water itself. Nothing broke the surface of the water up Spout Springs Hollow — no orchard of apple trees, no great sycamores sheltering the house, no roofline of house itself or barn. Nothing. The surface of the water was unruffled and still and placid. But as plain as I ever saw anything in my life, I saw the logs of this old house lying on the bottom, like broken ribs, drowned far below.

It has been a while since we learned. We have grown a little used to our pain, to living with it, sort of shifting under it so it can be borne. But we haven't enough years left ever to outgrow it.

We built this house ourselves. There was no contractor, no middleman. There was just Mister G. and his cousin and a good friend. It was built for two particular people with their particular needs in mind, and their labor and their love and even their tears went into its building. By the time it is drowned we will have lived in it several years. Long enough to have made it a home and for a lot of living to have been done, but we meant it for the rest of our lives.

In the time since we have learned our probable doom — we still hope, of course, it will pass us by — I have found myself often wandering from room to room, just looking at the old logs, maybe touching them, remembering, remembering . . .

Remembering when we found this set of logs for the kitchen. Remembering when we found that set of logs for the bedroom. Remembering that the set of logs which make the big living room was a Negro church. Remembering Mister G.'s father riving out our shingles. Remembering that every 2 x 4, every rafter, every length of studding and framing for the middle section came from our own timber. Remembering that the twelve smoked beams in the kitchen came from a house Mister G.'s great-great-uncle built a hundred and twenty years ago and still bear the mark of his broadax. Remembering that the mellow poplar of my kitchen cupboards also came from his old house and were first planed by his hand, made like satin later by Mister G.'s hand. Remembering that this house was a life's dream made real. Remembering, and beginning to say goodbye.

I do these things secretly, when Mister G. is not here, and I do what crying I do secretly also. He has his own grief to carry and it is much, much greater than mine, for he is losing not only the home he built, but his very country itself. The first Giles, Alexander, came to this piece of Green River in 1803 and Gileses have been here ever since. Nothing will remain of it that remotely resembles what Mister G. and all those generations have always known. There will be nothing left here for Mister G.

How do you reorient the heart?

We determined to set it all down, the story of a house conceived in nostalgia, born in hope, nurtured in determination, nourished in love, vexations, frustrations, joy, laughter, and triumph, matured in despair, and doomed by progress.

We don't know how much time we have left. We pray daily for a miracle. But it may be that like the old Negro singer we "ain't got time to fix the shingles, ain't got time to fix the door." We may have to move on and leave this old house behind.

We mean to leave it an epitaph.